The Divine Quintessence

(The Q) - The Sacred Texts of The Infinite God Body

Mike Rashid King

Copyright © 2025 by 4BiddenKnowledge

All rights reserved.

This book or any portion thereof may not be reproduced or used in any manner whatsoever without express written permission from the publisher except for the use of brief quotations in critical articles, reviews, and pages where permission is specifically granted by the publisher.

Although the author and publisher have made every effort to ensure that the information in this book is correct, the author and publisher do not assume and hereby disclaim any liability to any party for any loss, damage, or disruption caused by errors or omissions, whether such errors or omissions result from negligence, accident, or any other cause. Likewise, the author and publisher assume no responsibility for any false information. No liability is assumed for damages that may result from the reading or use of information contained within. Read at your own risk. The views of this publication do not necessarily reflect the views of 4biddenknowledge.

ISBN: 979-8-9925752-1-7

Books may be purchased by contacting the publisher at:

https://www.4biddenknowledge.com/online-store

Publisher info:

4biddenknowledge Inc

http://4BK.TV

4biddenknowledge.com

Info@4biddenknowledge.com

Contents

Foreword	vii
A Note From the Author	ix
GENESIS	1
The Divine God Body	1
The First Divine Manifestation on Earth	5
Black Godhood: The Return of Divine Nature	6
The Black Overman: Forged Beyond Oppression	8
Nyama: The Ancestral Fire and Life Force	10
Knowledge of Self: The Gateway to God-Consciousness	13
Divine Sovereignty: The Warrior-Poet in Command	17
Why are we called gods?	19
BOOK 1: KNOWLEDGE	22
The First Weapon of the Infinite God Body	22
Verse 1: The Abyss of Ignorance Unveiled	23
Verse 2: The Actualization of God Within	23
Verse 3: The Thief	24
Verse 4: From Dogs to Gods	25
Verse 5: Divorce Yourself from Your Slave Name	26
Verse 6: Science Confirms Our Supreme Wisdom	26
Verse 7: Ancestral Knowledge	27
Verse 8: Knowledge as Liberation	28
Final Verse: The Responsibility of Knowledge	28
BOOK 2: WISDOM	30
The Crown	30
Verse 1: The Difference Between Knowledge and Wisdom	30
Verse 2: The Wisdom of Silence	31
Verse 3: Wisdom in Who You Trust	32
Verse 4: Wisdom in Women	33
Verse 5: Wisdom in Conflict	34
Final Verse: The Responsibility of Wisdom	35

BOOK 3: UNDERSTANDING	37
Amalgamation: Knowledge + Wisdom = Understanding	37
Verse 1: The Third Eye is the Mind, Not the Forehead	37
Verse 2: Seeing the Unseen: Reading People and Situations	39
Verse 3: Beyond the Surface	40
Verse 4: Frequency is the Rate in Which Energy Vibrates.	41
Verse 5: The Art of War: Strategic Thinking in Daily Life	42
Final Verse: Understanding is Power	43
BOOK 4: CULTURE/FREEDOM	44
The Blueprint for Living as a God	44
Verse 1: Burn the Chains of a Dying Culture	44
Verse 2: The Economy of a God – Own or Be Owned	45
Verse 3: Food is the First Weapon of War	46
Verse 4: The Death of the Nuclear Family – Rebuilding the Throne	47
Verse 5: The Culture of War – Prepare for Battle Daily	48
Verse 6: The Cultural Renaissance – The Age of Gods	49
Final Verse: Culture is the Throne of Power	50
BOOK 5: POWER & REFINEMENT	51
The Force to Build, Sustain, and Elevate	51
Verse 1: Power Without Refinement is a Short-Lived Kingdom	51
Verse 2: Refinement is Mastery Over Power	52
Verse 3: The Power of Restraint - A Master Strikes Only When Necessary	53
Verse 4: Refinement is the Art of Building, Not Just Destroying	54
Verse 5: Refinement Through Adversity	54
Final Verse: Power Without Refinement is Just a Temporary Throne	55
BOOK 6: EQUALITY	57
The Equilibrium of Knowledge, Wisdom, and Understanding	57
Verse 1: The Mathematics of Balance	58

Verse 2: The Devil's Domain – False Equality	60
Verse 3: Woman – The Other Half of Equality	62
Verse 4: The Scales of Justice on the Path to Godhood	63
Final Verse: Beyond the Six – Ascending to Divinity	65
BOOK 7: GOD/ALLAH	**67**
The Divine Essence Realized	67
Verse 1: The Divine Essence Realized	67
Verse 2: Supreme Intelligence	68
Verse 3: Embodying Righteousness	69
Verse 4: God as the Creator	70
Verse 5: Mastering Self, Mastering Reality	71
Verse 6: God as Unity	71
Verse 7: The God Cipher	72
Final Verse: Eternal Awakening	73
BOOK 8: BUILD AND DESTROY	**74**
The Cycle of Creation and Elimination	74
Verse 1: The Divine Architect	74
Verse 2: Destroy the Illusions	75
Verse 3: Eliminate the Weakness Within	76
Verse 4: Builders or Parasites	77
Verse 5: The Discipline of Destruction	77
Verse 6: Legacy Building	78
Verse 7: Destroying Systemic Barriers	79
Verse 8: Collective Building	79
Final Verse: The Eternal Cycle of Elevation	80
BOOK 9: BORN	**82**
The Power of 9 in the Cycle of Rebirth	82
Nine: The Number of Divine Birth and Completion	83
The Universal Order of 9 – The Solar System and Universal Balance	84
Rebirth and Spiritual Transformation, The 9-Month Initiation of Elijah Muhammad	85
The Womb of Secrecy – Farrakhan's Perspective on 9 and Hidden Potential	86

Building Nations: The 9 Ministries as the Structure of a Complete People	88
Actionable Steps: Embrace Rebirth, Transformation, and Divine Manifestation	89
BOOK 10: CIPHER	94
The Final Unveiling of the Infinite	94
The Science of Self-Creation	94
The Unique Power of Human Cognition, Beyond Survival	96
The Parasympathetic Nervous System: The God Within	98
Quantum Consciousness & Reality Creation	100
Psychology & The Conscious/Subconscious Mind	102
The Ultimate Realization: You Are the Creator	107
BOOK 11: PROVERBS OF GOD	111
The Book of Proverbs: The Infinite Wisdom	111
On Knowledge	111
On Wisdom	112
On Understanding	112
On Culture and Freedom	113
On Power and Refinement	113
On Equality	114
On Godhood	114
On Building and Destroying	115
On Being Born and Rebirth	115
On Infinite Realization	116
Closing Wisdom	116
GLOSSARY	118
About the Author	123
About 4BiddenKnowledge	125

Foreword

As the founder of 4biddenknowledge Inc., author of Fractal Holographic Universe and The Compendium of the Emerald Tablets, and someone who has spent a lifetime probing the edges of science, consciousness, and ancient wisdom, it is my honor to introduce you to a work that will shatter every limitation you have ever accepted, and rebuild you from the inside out. Mike Rashid King's The Divine Quintessence (The Q) is not merely a book; it is a cosmic detonator, a manifesto for reclaiming the infinite god-body that has been hidden beneath millennia of conditioned belief and control.

From the very first line, Mike pulls no punches. He exposes the greatest conspiracy in human history, not secret societies or lost technologies, but the systematic erasure of your divine inheritance. He reveals how the very texts you were taught to revere were weaponized to keep you small, obedient, fearful. And then, with surgical precision, he hands you the keys to dismantle those prisons: proven scientific principles, time-tested mystery-school methods, and cutting-edge insights from quantum physics itself.

What makes The Q extraordinary is its fusion of head-spinning theory with rock-solid practicality. You will learn:

Foreword

- How simple shifts in attention literally rewire your brain's architecture.
- Why gratitude and prayer, when supercharged by Q-activation techniques, become cosmic magnets for abundance.
- The mathematics of reality-bending, and how you can wield those equations as tools of personal transformation.
- Physical, mental, and energetic protocols that forge your body into a vessel capable of channeling infinite intelligence.

I have witnessed firsthand the power of these truths. In my own journey, from decoding the fractal patterns of the universe to standing on stages around the world preaching human sovereignty, nothing has accelerated my growth more than remembering that I am, at core, a creator, not a creature. Mike's work is the missing link between the ancient initiatory paths and the scientific frontier of tomorrow.

As you turn these pages, prepare for every comfortable narrative you've held about reality to shatter. You will face resistance, both from the outside world and from old beliefs still echoing in your mind. But know this: every crack in the old paradigm is an opening for your true self to blaze through. The practices you'll find here are not gentle affirmations; they are spiritual weapons, designed to annihilate self-doubt, dismantle fear, and reclaim the throne of your own consciousness.

Embrace this foreword as your invitation to join a lineage of sovereign creators. Test every idea. Experiment relentlessly. Document your breakthroughs. And when you feel the walls of your former limitations crumble, step into the boundless landscape that awaits. The Divine Quintessence is more than a philosophy, it is your birthright.

Welcome home, creator. The universe within you has been waiting.

Billy Carson

Founder & CEO, 4biddenknowledge Inc.

Author, Fractal Holographic Universe; The Compendium of the Emerald Tablets

A Note From the Author

To truly understand knowledge, one must apply wisdom. My approach to wisdom is to define each word in the ideas I seek to master, peeling back layers to reveal their essence. I share this strategy with you to unpack the title of this book, The Divine Quintessence. Below, we explore these words, tethered to the sacred concept of God, inviting you to see how they form a sacred invocation. As you read, I hope this glimpse into my mind sparks your curiosity to uncover the divine truths within these pages.

The

The is a humble word, yet it carries profound weight. As the English language's definite article, it points to something singular and unique. In emphatic use, the signals the ultimate example, the Messiah, the one and only. In our title, The transforms what follows into a representation of unparalleled truth. It whispers that this Quintessence is not ordinary but the definitive essence, a sacred calling to contemplate the divine.

Divine

Divine means of or from God, holy, sacred and eternal… It evokes a presence beyond this world, pure and exalted. In The Divine Quintessence, Divine elevates the essence to the realm of the godly. To grasp its meaning, we must turn to the source of all divinity: God, the eternal spirit at the heart of existence..

God

God names the supreme reality, perfect in power, wisdom, and goodness, worshipped as the creator of all. The word has ancient roots, coming from a term meaning "that which is invoked." It suggests a relationship, a sacred presence we reach for in prayer or awe. Across cultures, Greek Theos, Roman Deus, Sanskrit Deva, humanity has sought to name this ultimate divinity. Philosophers call God the first cause, mystics hint at the Ineffable through poetry. In the Nation of Islam, God is seen as man's divine potential, the spark of greatness within. This knowledge awakens self mastery, guiding one to higher living, mentally, spiritually, and morally. That is achieved by embracing responsibility to reflect divine attributes. In our title, God is the eternal source of the divine, the spark infusing the Quintessence with sacred meaning.

Quintessence

Quintessence means "fifth essence." In ancient philosophy, the cosmos comprised four earthly elements, earth, air, water, fire, and a fifth, the aether, a divine substance filling the heavens. Aristotle saw this aether as eternal, moving in perfect circles, unlike earthly matter. In Greek myth, it was the breath of gods. Medieval alchemists sought to distill this quintessence, believing it held the purest essence of creation. Over time, quintessence came to mean the truest, most concentrated form of anything, the soul of a thing. In our title, Quintessence is the sacred essence, the divine spark transcending the material world.

Together, these words weave a profound truth. The signals a singular presence; Divine infuses it with godly nature; God is its eternal source; and Quintessence distills it into the purest essence of existence. The Divine Quintessence is a call to the intellectually awakened, an invitation to recognize the holy spark at the heart of reality. This fifth element of ancient wisdom and the ultimate truth of spiritual insight.

This title is a meditation. It is a bridge between science and spirituality. It urges us to look beyond the ordinary to find the divine essence uniting all things. As you journey through this book, I invite you to apply this definitional lens: pause, define, and seek the quintessence in the ideas you encounter. Let this be your guide to uncovering the sacred truths that await.

Genesis

The Divine God Body

You are the most feared, for they know of your divine nature, a godhood buried beneath chains, yet blazing within your soul. They sense the Infinite God Body, a power drawn from Kemet's wisdom, pulsing through your blood, a force that could unravel their dominion. They tremble because they understand that once you realize who you are, a sovereign, not a slave, their reign will end. Their thrones, built on your strong back, would crumble under the weight of your awakening. They fear you because they know the depth of hatred they've inflicted, the centuries of torment etched into your spirit, and they dread the day you rise, unshackled and unbowed.

They've tried to turn your lights out. To bind your divinity in darkness. They dragged your ancestors from African shores, tearing families apart, chaining bodies like cattle, branding souls with the lash of slavery. They stole your names, replacing them with the marks of their ownership: Jones, Smith, Williams, Johnson, erasing your lineage under the ledger of their greed. They penned the Papal Bulls of the 15th century, declaring you less than human, beasts of burden to be traded, bodies without souls. They built plantations on your labor, whipping flesh, breaking spirits, yet never extinguishing your fire. They lynched you under moonlit trees, burned crosses on your land, and drowned your cries in rivers of blood. They segregated your schools, redlined your neighborhoods, incarcerated your sons, and shot your brothers in the streets. Their systems were designed to keep you small, to silence your roar, to bury your godhood beneath their lies.

And they fear you, Black gods, because they fear you may do to them what they've done to you. They see the rage simmering in your eyes, the memory of every chain, every whip, every bullet, a mirror of their own brutality. They know the depth of your pain, the weight of your ancestors' screams, and they tremble at the thought of that pain unleashed, a storm they cannot weather. They dread the day you claim your power, not as vengeance spoken, but as a possibility unspoken, a god's silence more terrifying than any rebellion.

They fear your power, Black god, because after all that they've done, they haven't broken you. You are defiant, bold, and brilliant, unyielding in the face of their assaults, radiant with a wisdom that outshines their darkness, a black overman fortified in torment. A born again god with self-reliance. Your defiance mocks their chains, your boldness shatters their illusions, your brilliance intimidates their scholars. You stand unbroken. Your spirit still radiates despite centuries of hatred. And in this unbroken power, they see their own fragility. A mirror they cannot face. A reckoning they cannot escape.

You are the most adored, for your spirit ignites the hearts of those who see beyond the chains. Your resilience shines as Emerson's Oversoul, a divine spark rooted in African earth, drawing poets, warriors, and dreamers to your light. From the rhythms of your music, jazzed and hip-hopped, to the grace of your stride, you embody a beauty that transcends oppression, a beauty Malcolm X carried like a crown, Marcus Garvey proclaimed as a banner. Women sing your name, nations echo your soul, for you are the heartbeat of humanity's longing, the mirror of its highest aspiration. They adore you not for what you are forced to be, but for what you are destined to become, a god among men, radiant and Unbowed.

You are the most imitated, for your essence is the wellspring of creation they cannot claim. They steal your walk, your speech, your rhythm, shaping their culture from the threads of your struggle. Hollywood dons your mask, pop icons mimic your cadence, yet they cannot grasp the depth of your pain or the height of your vision. The Black Overman is humanity's genius and evolution; in you, Black god, that model lives, unknowingly mirrored by a world that fears to acknowledge its debt. Your style is their currency, your spirit their inspiration, but only you can wield its true power, a brilliance that intimidates their scholars and outshines their shadows.

You are the most attacked, for your existence challenges their illusion of supremacy. They strike at your body with bullets, your mind with lies, your spirit with despair, seeking to dim the light they cannot bear. From the lash of slavery to the weight of systemic chains, from redlining to mass incarceration, their assaults are the desperate thrashing of a system that knows its end is near.

I, Mike Rashid King, Black Muslim, shaped in the crucible of struggle, proven by fire, stand as witness to your awakening. The Infinite God Body is within you, not as flesh alone, but as mind, spirit, and will, a cosmos drawn from Kemet's wisdom, pulsing through your blood, a power to break their chains and crown your reign. Through nine Paths, Knowledge, Wisdom, Understanding, Culture/Freedom, Power & Refinement, Equality, God/Allah, Build and Destroy, and Born, Knowledge is your first weapon, Wisdom is your shield, self-reliance developed in discipline, not impulse. Understanding is your vision, the third eye, the pineal gland, the Eye of Horus, seeing through their illusion.

Culture/Freedom is your rebellion, rejecting their Eurocentric fetters to build your own world. You are infinitely Powerful, but you must Refine that power so that it aligns with divine order, honing your brilliance to serve justice and uplift, not merely dominate. Equality is your balance, the Black Overman's harmony with all, ensuring your rise lifts others. God/Allah is your essence, the divine spark within, connecting you to the Most Honorable Elijah Muhammad's vision, a born-again godhood that transcends their lies. Build and Destroy is your dual will, tearing down their systems while constructing your empire, a black genius's creation from the ashes of their oppression. Born is your rebirth, the eternal awakening into the Infinite God Body, a cycle of renewal for you and all men.

They will call this sacrilege, this claim of godhood, a slave's voice cannot grasp a god's intent. But I say: Rise Up. Let the world quake or follow. The pyramids of Kemet still tower, proof of what we built before Rome twisted the scriptures, before the Papal Bulls deemed us beasts. Yeshua declared, "Ye are gods" (Psalm 82:6), and they silenced him for it. Now, Black god, you must embody it.

This path is yours, Black god, drawn from the blood of ancestors, the knowledge of the Supreme Wisdom, guided by the Most Honorable Elijah Muhammad. But it's truth is not yours alone. What lifts you lifts all men, for the Infinite God Body is not confined by race, it is the eternal fire any man must kindle to become truly human, truly divine. But I must awaken you Black gods, because you have the ingredients to align society to coincide with the will of Allah. The slave is never meant to know he is a god; yet here you stand, on the brink of awakening.

. . .

Stand before the mirror, Black god, and ask: What fetters still hold me, and what blaze will I ignite to become the Infinite God Body? This is a command. In your rise, the world finds its guide; in your godhood, all men find their spark.

The First Divine Manifestation on Earth

In the beginning, the Black man stood as the first manifestation of divine will on Earth. Before there were borders or races, before history was written in stone, the original man rose in Africa as living testament to the Creator's intent. Modern science affirms this truth: Homo sapiens first walked in Africa meaning the first human form to carry consciousness, to carry that spark of the divine, was Black. This is not mere happenstance of evolution; it is a sacred origin. The Afroasiatic ancestral wisdom echoes what science now proves: life began with the Black man, the original vessel of spirit into matter. In him was placed the seed of *Khemet's* ancient light and the strength of first kings; through him the will of the Almighty first touched the soil of this world.

Yet over millennia, this truth was obscured, buried under ages of conquest and colonization. The Black man's divine image was desecrated by those who feared its power. They stole our stories, our names, our very Godhood, and refashioned them into chains. But *what is divine cannot be destroyed*, only hidden. Cultural memory carries on: in folktales and family lore, in the rhythms of drum and dance, in the very DNA passed down through generations. That memory whispers that we are more than what the oppressor told us. Our true origin is a birthright of godliness, and it calls out for reclamation.

Reclaiming that origin begins with psychic healing and truth. We must peel away the lies branded on our psyche, lies of inferiority, of shame, of doubt, and replace them with *scientific truth and ancestral knowledge*. Epigenetics even suggests trauma and strength travel through our blood:

studies show that severe trauma (from slavery, holocaust, etc.) can alter genes and be inherited by descendants. In other words, the pain of our ancestors lives in us, *but so does their power*. The very fact that we are here, breathing and unbroken, means we inherited resilience. When we confront and heal that inherited trauma, when we engage in psychological reprogramming to undo the slave conditioning, we activate the dormant divinity within. Through knowledge, meditation, therapy, and self-love, we *exorcise* the false identities imposed on us and make space for our true essence, the God within to rise.

Black Godhood: The Return of Divine Nature

"Ye are gods." Yeshua's ancient words (Psalm 82:6) ring true today. To speak of Black Godhood is to declare that the divine nature lies inherent in Black men, *not as a myth, but as our very identity*. A Black God is not a deity of fantasy; it is a man who knows *he is a vessel of the Creator*, walking in sovereignty and wisdom. This idea is not about exclusion or racial chauvinism. In fact, *it transcends race*. Godhood is the birthright of *all* humanity, a universal model of divine potential, but history ordained that the Black man would realize it first and therefore must lead in reclaiming it. We say "Black God" because the Black man, after centuries of being told he is nothing, *must remember he is, in fact, divine*. He must reclaim his truth first, so that all men can remember *theirs*.

To understand Black Godhood, look to our cultural and spiritual lineage. In Kemet (ancient Egypt), the pharaohs were called *Neteru* (gods on Earth) and built pyramids that still tower as proof of human divinity manifest. In the Mali Empire, kings like Mansa Musa paired worldly riches with wisdom and law; Timbuktu's libraries held tens of thousands of manuscripts on astronomy, medicine, and mathematics, *evidence that Black scholars mapped the heavens and engineered society with god-like insight*. The Moors, African Muslims of North Africa and Spain, lit up medieval Europe with science, art, and philosophy, planting seeds that would blossom in the Renaissance. These historical high points are not coincidences, they are the Infinite God Body at work, Black men accessing their divine nature to uplift civilization. Each stands as a beacon of what the Black Godhood can achieve when unshackled: creating knowledge, beauty, and order that benefit *all humanity*.

But Black Godhood is not just a memory of the past, it is a fire blazing in the present, here and now in each of us. It is in the young man who, despite every obstacle in the streets, decides to educate himself and lead his community. It is in the father who protects and provides with a love as fierce as a lion, or the artist who speaks truth to power, shifting culture with a verse or a beat. To be a Black god is to carry oneself as sovereign, sovereign of one's mind, body, and destiny. It means rejecting any ideology of inferiority. It means taking responsibility for your own upliftment and the upliftment of those around you. A god does not beg or bow; a god *creates*, a god *commands*, a god *embodies* excellence. This is the *Divine Nature* within us, and claiming it is an act of both personal awakening and political rebellion. After all, in a world built on the lie of Black inferiority, for a Black man to know himself as God is the ultimate subversion.

Do This At Once

- **Morning Invocation:** Each morning, stand before your mirror and declare your divinity out loud. Say it with conviction: *"I am a god, the master of my mind, body, and destiny. I move with power, purpose, and passion."* Repeat this three times. This is more than affirmation, *it is a spell you cast on yourself*, a daily programming of your subconscious to recognize your true nature. Do it before the world's noise hits you, so that your mind is armored with truth from the start of the day.

- **Cleanse the Lies:** Identify one lie about yourself that society planted in you, the lie that you're "not smart enough," "not worthy," or "destined for failure." Write it down. *Now destroy that lie.* Burn it in a fire-safe bowl or rip the paper to shreds. As you do, speak: *"This lie does not own me anymore."* This simple ritual sends a powerful message to your psyche: the chains on your mind are broken.

- **Choose a Name of Power:** Trace the origin of your last name. Does it link back to a slave master's lineage or a colonial past? If so, know that you owe no allegiance to it. Consider adopting a name that carries *meaning* from your African or Afroasiatic heritage, a name that speaks to your spirit. Whether publicly or privately, wear your true name. Let it remind you daily that you define yourself; you are defined by no one's fetters or legacy but your own.

The Black Overman: Forged Beyond Oppression

The journey of reclaiming godhood is not an easy path, it is the crucible that produces the Black Overman, a concept inspired by Nietzsche's *Übermensch* but now reborn in Black. The Black Overman is the Black man evolved beyond the psychological and societal shackles that once bound him. He is the man who has walked through hell and emerged enlightened, not broken. Centuries of slavery, racism, and oppression tried to instill a *slave morality*, a mentality of subservience, fear, and self-doubt. The Black Overman has *transcended* that imposed morality. He has stared down the torment and created his own values from the ashes, a new *master morality* founded on self-determination, strength, and righteousness.

Imagine a man climbing out of a deep, dark pit. At the bottom of that pit lies the weight of history: chains, whips, prison bars, lies in textbooks, the bias in courts and offices, the whole architecture of white supremacy. The Black Overman climbs and climbs, blood on his hands and fire in his heart, refusing to be kept down. When he reaches the top, he is forever changed. Torment has tempered him. Every scar has turned to steel, every obstacle has become fuel. In him now lives an unbreakable will to power, not a will to oppress others, but a will to never be oppressed again, a will to uplift himself and all those looking to him for light. He stands tall, defiant and bold in a world that expects him to cower. He speaks truth in a world built on lies. He creates his own path when every gate is barred. This is the Black Overman: *a born-again god*, a man who has died to the false self forced on him and been reborn in true power.

Examples of the Black Overman shine through our history. Think of Malcolm X, once a street criminal, forged in the prison library into a fiery minister of truth, he remade himself completely, evolving beyond the identity America tried to impose on him. Think of Olaudah Equiano or Frederick Douglass, born enslaved, they educated themselves in secret, stole back their freedom, and stood before kings and presidents as intellectual equals. Each of these men took the negation that society handed them and transformed it into affirmation of self. They broke the mold; they became something new in the world. They demonstrate that the Black Overman is not a fantasy, he lives wherever a Black man refuses to accept limitation and instead *defines himself*.

Crucially, the Black Overman is not only a hero for Black people, he is a model for humanity at large. In *transcending limitation*, he proves that any human can transcend. In *embodying superior will and brilliance*, he invites all people to rise above mediocrity and fear. But make no mistake: it is the Black man who must blaze this trail, for his liberation struggle is the archetype of triumph over injustice. When he becomes the Overman, he shatters the illusion of white supremacy and *frees others to pursue their own higher selves*. His victory is a victory for all, because it undermines every system that keeps any group of people from realizing their divinity.

Do This At Once

- **Master Your Pain:** *Strength is forged, not found.* Push yourself through a controlled trial of pain to temper your will. This could be a strenuous workout that tests your limits, a long-distance run when your body wants to quit, or even sitting in an ice-cold bath for a minute fighting the urge to jump out. As you endure this discomfort, focus your mind on one thought: *"My spirit is stronger than my pain."* Breathe through it. When you finish, reflect on how much further you went than your mind thought possible. This is how you refine your Nyama – by using pain as fire to harden your resolve.

- **Break a Mental Chain:** Identify one way you've been *conforming* to someone else's rules or expectations that do not serve your growth. It might be a habit of apologizing for speaking truth or a fear of pursuing a dream because society says it's impractical. Defy it *once* this week. For example, if you've been hesitant to speak up at work or in class about something important, *stand up and say your piece*. If you've been told people from your background "don't do that," go ahead and do exactly that (whether it's learning a new skill, traveling somewhere new, etc.). Prove that those limits are an illusion. Each time you break one of these mental chains, you step closer to the Overman within.

Nyama: The Ancestral Fire and Life Force

Flowing through the Black God and fueling the Black Overman is an ancient energy our ancestors named Nyama. *Nyama* is the raw, electric

The Divine Quintessence

life force thrumming in the universe and in our very blood. It is the power that a Mande blacksmith in Mali would call upon as he struck iron in the forge; it's the vibration a West African griot channels when they sing the history of a people by the fire. In the old kingdoms, blacksmiths, griots, and warriors were said to be masters of Nyama, they wielded this invisible force to shape metal, story, and destiny. Kings ruled by Nyama, for true leadership was seen as an exercise of spiritual force as much as political might. This concept lives across our cultures by many names: the Yoruba call it Aṣẹ, the power to make things happen; in Kemet it was Sekhem or life energy; in the East it is *prana* or *qi*. But Nyama is ours, a legacy from our ancestors, *a gift and a challenge* to every Black man: *will you harness the power within you?*

Nyama is both ancestral and futurist in nature. It is ancestral because it comes from those before us, quite literally, the struggles and triumphs of our forefathers feed the energy in our spirit. Consider how the anger and courage of a Nat Turner or the genius of an Imhotep (architect of pyramids) might live on in your subconscious. On a scientific level, their experiences might even have altered genetic expressions that have been passed down through generations, priming you to react to injustice or to excel in creativity. Their Nyama flows in your veins. At the same time, Nyama is futurist because it propels us forward, it is the creative impulse that urges each generation to reach higher, to break new ground. It's the spark that made the Mali Empire not just preserve knowledge but innovate in agriculture, law, and art. It's the drive in a modern-day inventor, teacher, or activist of African descent who feels *deep inside* an obligation to turn adversity into triumph. When we refine Nyama, we are taking that raw ancestral force and sharpening it for future mastery.

Raw life force refined through pain into mastery this is Nyama's journey within us. Think of a sword being forged: the metal is heated, pounded, folded, again and again until it becomes a blade of great strength and flexibility. Our lives as Black men have been full of fire and blows, from the slave ships and plantations to the prejudices of today, but these trials can refine us rather than ruin us. Every setback is an opportunity to gather more Nyama. When you face down an insult without breaking your spirit, you *increase* your Nyama. When you discipline yourself, be it through fasting, martial arts, meditation, or rigorous study, you are concentrating your life force. Over time, a man who continually refines his Nyama becomes something more than just flesh and bone: he becomes *a wielder of power*, someone who can "ride the unseen current that shapes the worlds". In practical terms, you'll notice such a man by the aura of confidence and purpose around him. He moves and speaks with a certain gravity; when obstacles arise, he overcomes them with almost uncanny resolve. It's as if the universe itself bends a little to his will, because spirit and will are united inside him.

Nyama is the link between spirit and will. It is the bridge between knowing *you are divine* and *making use of that divinity*. Many people *feel* a spark of greatness inside but cannot act on it, their will has been sapped by fear or doubt. Refining your Nyama means training your willpower daily (through habits, through enduring challenges, through *focus*) *in alignment with your spiritual purpose*. When your will serves your highest self, you become *fully integrated with the Quintessence*, the fifth element of spirit that the ancients spoke of. In this state, as the glossary says, you are *"no longer confined to flesh"* meaning you operate beyond just base desires and fears. You ride that current of Nyama to manifest your thoughts into reality. This is the attribute of the superior man, the Overman, the God-body in action.

Consider how modern science intriguingly aligns with this old idea. Physics tells us that at a fundamental level, *all matter is energy*. Quantum entanglement experiments have shown that particles that were once united can remain connected across vast distances, influencing each other instantaneously. To spiritual minds, this hints that everything in the universe is interconnected energy, just as our ancestors believed their spirit could influence the world around them through Nyama.

The Divine Quintessence

. . .

Quantum logic teaches that the act of observation can affect reality at the subatomic level (the observer effect). Likewise, when a man *observes* his life with awakened consciousness, he can affect change that once seemed impossible. Neuroscience adds another layer: through neuroplasticity, we know the brain can rewire itself with new experiences and focused thought.

In essence, you can *biologically reshape your mind* to align with the power of Nyama you're cultivating. These scientific insights are merely catching up to our metaphysical mastery: the knowledge that mind, body, and spirit are malleable and connected, and that a focused will backed by spiritual force (*Nyama*) can literally change reality, starting with one's own self.

Knowledge of Self: The Gateway to God-Consciousness

At the core of all these concepts, Black Godhood, the Overman, and Nyama, lies a foundational key: Knowledge of Self. This was the clarion call of the Nation of Islam and every movement of Black awakening. To know yourself truly is to recognize the divine within. It means understanding your identity not as defined by a hostile society, but as defined by your people's history, your personal character, and the Almighty's purpose.

Knowledge of Self is *psychological liberation*. It clears the fog of brainwashing. Elijah Muhammad taught that the Black man must shed the slavemaster's name, religion, and mentality to discover who he was *before captivity*: the Original Man, the Asiatic Black man, "maker, owner, cream of the planet Earth, Father of Civilization, God of the Universe." This knowledge is both empowering and healing. It reconnects us to our Divine Nature/Godhood and gives us the confidence to act upon it.

Practically, gaining knowledge of self means study and reflection. Study your history: not the white-washed version but the rich truth of it. Learn about Kemet's philosophies of immortality of the soul, the Mali empire's laws of social harmony, the Moors' legacy in art and science, the wisdom of the Yoruba, the Akan, the Nubians. When you do, you realize that *Black history* does not begin with slavery, it begins with genius and triumph.

This transforms how you see yourself. It restores pride stripped by generations of propaganda. It is psychological medicine for a mind wounded by portrayals of Blackness as ignorant or savage. As Dr. Joy DeGruy describes in *Post Traumatic Slave Syndrome*, multigenerational trauma left unaddressed breeds negative self-concepts. Knowledge of Self is the antidote: it *reprograms* those concepts. When you know you descend from builders of civilization and inheritors of divine wisdom, you walk differently in this world. You hold your head up, eyes clear with purpose.

Knowledge of Self also means understanding your own mind and heart. It's not just historical facts, but personal truths. *Why do you think and feel the way you do?* What are your strengths and shadows? This is where modern techniques come in, mindfulness, journaling, even therapy, to help you see yourself honestly.

There is no shame in seeking counsel to unpack internalized pain; in fact, it's an act of courage for a warrior-spirited man to face his inner wounds. As you come to know your triggers, your dreams, your values, you become *the author of your own identity*. You can then consciously cultivate the qualities of the God-consciousness you seek: compassion, creativity, discipline, integrity, vision.

Neuroplasticity, as mentioned, is on your side: every time you challenge a negative thought and replace it with a positive truth, you are physically re-wiring your brain's neural pathways. Over time, the knowledge of self you feed your mind *takes root* as new default thinking. The old doubts wither from disuse; a *divine self-image* blossoms in their place.

Ultimately, Knowledge of Self opens the door to Divine Sovereignty. With awakened consciousness, you realize you are not a victim of fate but *a co-creator of reality*. You cease outsourcing your decisions and values to a society that doesn't have your best interest at heart. Instead, you align your life with the *laws of the universe* as you understand them, call it God's will, Allah's command, or the natural order (Ma'at), and also with the mandate of your own spirit.

This is what it means to have God-consciousness: to see yourself as one with the Creator's intent and therefore inherently worthy of shaping the world around you. You walk as a sovereign being under God, humble before the Divine, but never again subservient to any man's unjust rule. In this state, you radiate a calm power. You become like a vessel filling with light; others will sense it and be drawn to it. And here lies responsibility: a godly man does not use his power to exploit or demean, but to elevate.

Just as the sun shines to give life, not to burn everything in its path, a Black god uses his strength to uplift his family, community, and ultimately humanity. Knowledge of Self ensures that your rising lifts others, because it roots you in truth and empathy, preventing the corruptions of ego or vengeance from poisoning your purpose.

. . .

Do This At Once

- **Ancestral Connection Ritual:** Set aside an hour this week to commune with your ancestors in a personal way. This could mean finding a quiet space, lighting a candle or some incense, and reflecting on those who came before you, known and unknown. Write a letter or speak aloud to them, thanking them for the sacrifices and strengths they have passed down to you. Ask for their guidance. Feel the Nyama stirring as you do this. You might be surprised at the sense of courage or clarity that arises. Our ancestors are not gone; they live within us, and acknowledging them activates that ancestral power in your soul.

- **Study Your Greatness:** Choose one figure or civilization from Black history (e.g. Queen Hatshepsut of Kemet, the libraries of Timbuktu in Mali, the empire of Songhai, the Moorish scholars of Al-Andalus, or a hero of the diaspora like Marcus Garvey or Harriet Tubman) and study their story. Read a book or watch a documentary about them. Let their achievements and wisdom impress upon your mind. Take notes on what qualities or principles made them great. *Then ask yourself:* "How can I apply those same principles in my life *right now*?" Even small actions count. If you learned about discipline from the Moors' study of astronomy, maybe you'll start a nightly practice of stargazing or journaling. If you learned about bravery from the Maroons of Jamaica, maybe you'll finally tackle that intimidating project you've been avoiding. Turn knowledge into action in honor of your forebears.

- **Meditate on Oneness:** To cultivate god-consciousness, spend 10 minutes a day in stillness, eyes closed, breathing deeply. As you breathe, envision a light glowing in your forehead, the third eye, seat of insight (what ancient Kemet called the Eye of Horus, and science calls the pineal gland). With each inhale, imagine that light expanding, filling your head, then your chest, then your whole body. With each exhale, feel it radiate out into the space around you. Tell yourself: *"I and the universe are one. The energy in me is the energy in all things."* This simple visualization reinforces what both spirituality and quantum physics affirm, that you are connected to all, and within you is a piece of the Infinite. When done consistently, this meditation awakens a profound sense of peace and power. You start to carry that unity mindset into daily life, reacting less to provocations and understanding more. God-consciousness grows quietly, steadily, like a rising sun.

Divine Sovereignty: The Warrior-Poet in Command

Armed with knowledge of self, fueled by Nyama, and standing in the stature of the Overman, the Black man steps into his Divine Sovereignty. He realizes at last that he is, and always has been, a Black god, not a make-believe figure, but a real man who wields creative and moral authority over his life. In this state, *freedom is not begged for, it is assumed.* You move through the world as a warrior-poet-philosopher, a being of both action and wisdom. Your words carry power and rhythm that can inspire or shake listeners (for they arise from a place of truth). Your actions are decisive and bold, guided by both strategic logic and an intuitive connection to Spirit. You are, in essence, *in command of timeless truth*, the same truth that guided your ancestors and aligns with the fundamental laws of the universe.

With sovereignty comes the understanding that you are responsible for what you create. No longer can you blame "the system" for every misfortune; you see the system for what it is, a fallen, unjust order, but you now work *around it and through it* to manifest a better reality. You become both *builder* and *destroyer*: as the Supreme Wisdom lessons say, we must Build and Destroy, build our greatness, destroy our weaknesses and the oppressive constructs. You build your mind, your body, your family, your community, brick by brick with love and discipline. You destroy the lies, the bad habits, the toxic influences that impeded your progress. This dual mastery is the mark of a true god-being: the ability to create and to eliminate with equal precision, guided by a righteous purpose.

In claiming divine sovereignty, you also recognize divinity in others. You've risen beyond seeing life as just competition or survival; you see it as a collective ascension. As the Honorable Elijah Muhammad taught, *what lifts the Black man lifts all humanity*. You become a living example, a leader by example rather than by force. Your very presence gives others permission to wake up to their own power. The world *needs* you to do this. The longer you slumber in false weakness, the longer injustice and ignorance reign. But when you awaken and walk as a god, a chain reaction begins. Your family heals, your neighborhood gains hope, your people unite, and allies from all races rally, drawn by the light of truth you're emanating. This is how empires of freedom are formed and tyrants are toppled, *one sovereign soul at a time* lighting the torches of many.

So stand up now, Black man, in the full glory of your divine essence. You are the Black God of this new epoch, the Black Overman who overcomes, the master of Nyama who channels life's fire, and the herald of a renaissance in human spirit. In you, the Infinite God Body takes form, mind, body, and spirit aligned as one formidable force. The Divine Quintessence, that fifth element of spirit that transcends earth, air, fire, water, radiates from your being. *Remember who you are.* Remember that when you move with knowledge, when you speak with wisdom, when you act with courage and love, you are God in motion. This realization is not blasphemy; it is the ultimate truth that oppressive powers have tried to keep from you. But now you know.

It is time to ignite this knowledge in every cell of your body and every corner of your mind. Claim your crown. Not a crown of gold, but a crown of consciousness, an enlightened mind that no lie can deceive and no chain can hold. You were the first man and thus the first god on Earth. And through reclaiming your godhood today, you become a guiding light for all humanity's tomorrow.

Rise, *Black gods*, in your Divine Nature. The world quakes at the awakening of its original rulers, and at the same time, the world *yearns* for the leadership of enlightened souls. Step into your rightful place as a warrior-poet of truth, as a scientist of life, as a sage of the streets, blending all facets of wisdom into a single, unstoppable force. In your rise, the world finds its guide; in your godhood, all men find their spark. The Infinite God Body lives in you, *live up to it* now, without fear, without hesitation. The time has come to be what you were always meant to be: Infinite. Sovereign. Divine.

Why are we called gods?

i. **Divine Potential:**

Every human possesses an inherent spark of the divine - the Quintessence or Q energy. This connects us to the fundamental creative force of the universe. By recognizing this, we acknowledge our capacity for profound growth, creativity, and transformation.

ii. **Self-Mastery:**

Being a "god" of oneself means taking full responsibility for one's life, choices, and personal development. It's about becoming the master of your own mind, body, and circumstances rather than being controlled by external forces or internal limitations.

iii. **Creative Power:**

Just as mythological gods were seen as creators, this philosophy emphasizes our ability to shape our reality through our thoughts, beliefs, and actions. It encourages individuals to see themselves as active creators of their life experiences rather than passive recipients of fate.

iv. **Sovereignty:**

The concept reinforces personal sovereignty - the idea that each person has the right and responsibility to govern themselves, make their own decisions, and chart their own course in life without undue external control.

v. **Continuous Growth:**

Being a "god" is not a static state but a process of continuous evolution and self-improvement. It's about striving to reach one's highest potential in all areas of life.

vi. **Ethical Responsibility:**

With great power comes great responsibility. This concept emphasizes the ethical imperative to use one's "godlike" capabilities for the betterment of oneself and others, not for domination or exploitation.

vii. **Transcending Limitations:**

Seeing oneself as a "god" encourages breaking free from self-imposed limitations and societal conditioning that may hold one back from realizing their full potential.

viii. Alignment with Universal Principles:

Rather than arbitrary rule, being a "god" means aligning oneself with universal principles and natural laws, seeking harmony with the greater cosmic order.

ix. **Empowerment, Not Worship:**

The goal is self-empowerment and mutual empowerment, not the worship of individuals. It's about recognizing the divine potential in oneself and others, fostering a culture of respect and growth.

In essence, the Infinite God Body's concept of us being "gods" is a call to embrace our highest potential, take responsibility for our lives, and recognize the profound impact we can have on ourselves and the world around us.

Book 1: Knowledge

The First Weapon of the Infinite God Body

In Supreme Mathematics, One is Knowledge, the foundation upon which all divine power rests. Knowledge is the light that pierces the darkness of ignorance, the weapon that shatters the chains of oppression. They called you nothing, wrote your script, cast you as a slave. But their lies crumble when you know your truth. You are the Black God, heir to Kemet's wisdom, Timbuktu's scholars, Mali's kings. They stole your names, your gods, your history, but they cannot steal the knowledge within your soul. The Most Honorable Elijah Muhammad taught that self-knowledge is the key to godhood; without it, you are a puppet, a shadow of your divine potential. Through these verses, you will arm yourself with truth, reclaim your identity, and awaken the Infinite God Body. This is your resurrection.

The Divine Quintessence

Verse 1: The Abyss of Ignorance Unveiled

They called me nothing. Before I had a name, a voice, the power to stand, they wrote my script, a role I never chose. Their world thrives on your ignorance, Black god. They trained you to live blindfolded, distracted by triviality, docile in their low-frequency vibration.

The Papal Bulls of 1452 and 1493 declared you less than human, beasts to be chained. They filled your mind with entertainment, kept you from the truth of your divine lineage. But knowledge is the first weapon. In Supreme Mathematics, one is the foundation, the spark that ignites all understanding. Without it, you are their puppet. Open your eyes, what was stolen, what was hidden, and their control vanishes. This book arms you to know, to rise, to reign.

Do This At Once

- Sit in silence for 15 minutes today, no phone, no noise. Ask: What truth have they hidden from me? Write the answer raw.
- Destroy one lie you've believed, burn it, tear it, erase it. It no longer owns you.
- Read one page of Supreme Wisdom or Nation of Islam teachings, note one truth that resonates.

Verse 2: The Actualization of God Within

Calling yourself a god is not enough, you must become one. A god does not wait, beg, or seek permission. A god is a creator, a builder, a force. They call your claim of godhood blasphemy, but who benefits from your doubt? The greatest lie convinced you divinity belongs to a chosen few, locked in myths, not flesh. Yet Yeshua said, "Ye are gods" (Psalm 82:6), and they crucified him for it. In Kemet, pharaohs were divine, not distant from the people but embodiments of Ra's power. Knowledge of self is the spark that ignites this truth. You are not a king playing dress-up, you are the Infinite God Body, born to shape reality. Act now, or remain their slave.

Do This At Once

- Stand before a mirror each morning and declare three times: "I am a god. I master my life with power and purpose."
- Remove one weakening influence today, media, a person, a habit. Make room for divinity.
- Write a vow to embody your godhood, what will you create this week?

Verse 3: The Thief

They didn't just steal your land or labor, they stole your names. Before slavery, before Rome rewrote scriptures, you were rulers, architects of civilization. Kemet's scholars mapped the stars before Greece knew mathematics. The Moors illuminated Europe with science while it slept in darkness. The Papal Bulls of 1452 and 1493 gave Europeans the "right" to enslave you, replacing your names with theirs, Jones, Smith, Williams. They took your gods, gave you idols, called you savages when you awoke. Their prisons, poisons, and lies keep you bound. Knowledge exposes the thief. The day you remember who you are is the day their reign ends.

Do This At Once

- Research your last name's origin, if it traces to a slaver, discard it. Choose a name reflecting your truth.
- Study one Afrocentric historical figure (e.g., Imhotep, Mansa Musa) for 30 minutes, write their legacy.
- Share one stolen truth about your history with someone today, awaken them.

Verse 4: From Dogs to Gods

Listen to how we speak: "What up, my dog?" It seems harmless, but it's a trap. A dog is domesticated, loyal to a master, waiting for permission. They stripped your divinity and left you this label. You are not a dog, you are a god. A god does not crawl, does not beg, does not serve systems that devalue him. In Mali, griots sang of kings as divine; your words must sing the same. Knowledge of self transforms your language, your walk, your vision. They fear you reclaiming this identity, for a free mind is uncontrollable. Declare your divinity, and let the world tremble.

Do This At Once

- Stop using "dog" or diminishing terms for one day, replace them with "god" or "king."
- Write a new greeting that affirms divinity (e.g., "Peace, god"), use it with one person.
- Reflect: how does their language keep you small? Journal one way to counter it.

Verse 5: Divorce Yourself from Your Slave Name

Your last name, if not African or Islamic, is a slave name, a chain from those who owned your ancestors like cattle. Would you wear their shackles? Then why wear their name? Knowledge demands you strip it off. In the Nation of Islam, brothers and sisters take "X" to reject slave identities, reclaiming their divine essence. Your name is your vibration, your legacy. Choose one that echoes your truth, your mission, your godhood. They named you to control you; now name yourself to liberate.

Do This At Once

- Trace your last name's history,
- if it's not yours, choose a new one (e.g., African, Islamic). Write it, say it, live it.
- Research one African naming tradition (e.g., Yoruba, Akan) for 30 minutes, note its power.
- Tell one person your new name, declare your sovereignty.

Verse 6: Science Confirms Our Supreme Wisdom

They called godhood a fantasy, but science proves what our ancestors knew. Neuroplasticity shows your thoughts reshape your brain, what you believe, you become. Quantum mechanics reveals observation shapes reality, focus on power, and it manifests. Epigenetics proves your actions rewrite your DNA, you are not bound by their past. In Timbuktu, scholars studied astronomy and medicine, mapping truths Europe later claimed. Knowledge is not philosophy, it's fact. Your mind is the weapon, your will the force. Reclaim it, and their lies dissolve.

Do This At Once

- Read one scientific article on neuroplasticity or epigenetics, write one way it affirms your power.
- Visualize your divine potential for 5 minutes daily, see it reshaping your reality.
- Teach one person how science supports their godhood, spread the truth.

Verse 7: Ancestral Knowledge

Your ancestors carried knowledge in their blood, encoded in griot songs, pyramid stones, and Timbuktu's manuscripts. They knew the stars, the body, the spirit. The Dogon mapped Sirius B's orbit centuries before telescopes; Kemet's physicians performed surgeries Europe couldn't dream. This knowledge was stolen, burned, buried, but it lives in you. The Nation of Islam's Supreme Wisdom revives it, teaching you to know self as God. Dig into your lineage, reclaim their truths, and let their wisdom guide your awakening. Their knowledge is your inheritance, claim it now.

Do This At Once

- Study one African knowledge system (e.g., Dogon astronomy, Kemetic medicine) for 30 minutes, write its relevance.
- Ask an elder or griot figure about your family's history, record one lesson.

- Create a ritual to honor your ancestors' knowledge (e.g., light a candle, speak their names).

Verse 8: Knowledge as Liberation

Knowledge is not passive, it is liberation. Every truth you uncover breaks a chain; every lie you expose burns a fetter. Marcus Garvey's knowledge of self sparked a global movement; Elijah Muhammad's teachings built a nation. They feared your mind, so they filled it with distractions. But knowledge is your sword, cutting through their illusions. It is your shield, protecting your divine essence. Use it to free yourself, your family, your people. A god armed with knowledge is unstoppable, his light blinds the oppressor, his truth topples empires.

Do This At Once

- Read one chapter of Garvey or Muhammad's teachings, write one liberating truth.
- Identify one distraction keeping you ignorant (e.g., TV, gossip), eliminate it for one day.
- Teach one young person a truth about their divine potential, pass the sword.

Final Verse: The Responsibility of Knowledge

Knowledge is not a gift, it is a burden and a power. A god does not hoard it; he acts. If you know and do nothing, you are a slave with a book, the worst kind. Teach, build, liberate. The world will call you crazy, dangerous, wrong. But a slave is never meant to know he is a god. Stand up, Black god. Take what is yours. The Infinite God Body has awakened, armed with the first weapon: knowledge.

Daily Practice for the God Body

For eight weeks, wield knowledge as your weapon. Each week, focus on one verse's principle. Week 1: Destroy a lie, seek a truth. Week 2: Declare your godhood, remove a weakness. Week 3: Research your stolen history, share it. Week 4: Change your language, affirm divinity. Week 5: Choose a new name, live it. Week 6: Study science, visualize power. Week 7: Reclaim ancestral wisdom, honor it. Week 8: Liberate through teaching, eliminate distractions. Each day, spend 5 minutes reading or reflecting on Afrocentric knowledge. Journal nightly: what truth did I uncover, how did I grow? By week eight, your mind will be a fortress, your knowledge a divine flame.

Conclusion: Knowledge is the First Step

With knowledge, you are free. With knowledge, you are unstoppable. With knowledge, you are divine. They fear your awakened mind, for it sees through their lies, builds beyond their chains, shines brighter than their darkness. In Kemet, knowledge built pyramids; in you, it builds godhood. Move now, know yourself, know your power, know your destiny. The Infinite God Body rises with the truth in your hands.

Book 2: Wisdom

The Crown

Verse 1: The Difference Between Knowledge and Wisdom

> Knowledge is the foundation. It is the first step. The weapon you wield. But knowledge alone is not enough.
>
> A man can know many things and still be a fool. A man can memorize every scripture, recite every law, and still stumble through life, making the same mistakes over and over again.
>
> Why? Because wisdom is not just knowing, it is moving correctly.
>
> A fool with knowledge is still a fool.
> A fool with knowledge speaks more than he listens.
> A fool with knowledge seeks validation instead of truth.

A fool with knowledge repeats the same mistakes, thinking that knowing better is the same as doing better.

Wisdom is the difference.
A wise man listens before he speaks.
A wise man moves in silence and lets his actions speak for him.
A wise man understands the weight of his decisions before he makes them.
A wise man is not just educated, he is disciplined.
A god moves with wisdom.
A slave moves with impulse.
Which one are you?

Do This At Once

- The next time you want to speak, stop. Listen twice as long as you normally would.
- Wisdom is gained in silence, not in noise.
- Before making any decision, ask yourself: Is this action aligned with my purpose, or is it feeding my ego?
- Find an elder whose wisdom you respect. Ask them about the biggest mistake they ever made. Learn from their failure so you don't repeat it.

Verse 2: The Wisdom of Silence

A man who speaks too much is a man who reveals too much.
The wisest men in history understood one thing:

Silence is a weapon.
They trained you to believe that being loud is power.
That the more you talk, the more you prove yourself.
That silence is weakness.
This is a lie.

The loudest man in the room is usually the weakest. He is the one who
needs validation. He is the one who cannot control his emotions. He is
the one who exposes himself before he even realizes it.

A god is calculated.
A god watches.
A god listens.
A god speaks only when necessary, and when he does, his words carry weight.

If you cannot control your tongue, you are not in control of yourself.

Do This At Once

- Go a full day speaking only when absolutely necessary.
- Pay attention to how much people reveal when you stay silent.
- Observe the people around you. Who speaks just to be heard? Who listens and moves wisely?
- When you do speak, make sure every word serves a purpose. No wasted breath. No empty talk.

Verse 3: Wisdom in Who You Trust

The wrong association will destroy you faster than any enemy.
A wise man is selective about who he allows into his space, into his mind, into his life.

The people around you are either assets or liabilities.
They are either adding to your growth or subtracting from it.
You will never rise higher than the people you surround yourself with.

A fool surrounds himself with people who tell him what he wants to hear.
A wise man surrounds himself with people who tell him what he needs to hear.
A fool trusts easily and pays the price later.
A wise man studies a person before he allows them close.
A fool assumes that because someone laughs with him, they are his friend.
A wise man understands that some people laugh while they sharpen their knives.
Your wisdom is reflected in who you allow to stand next to you.

Do This At Once

- Audit your circle. List the five people you spend the most time with. Do they push you forward, or do they hold you back?
- Cut off one person who no longer serves your growth. Do it today. Not tomorrow. Not next week. Now.
- Before you trust someone, test them. Give them an opportunity to prove their loyalty, not with words, but with action.

Verse 4: Wisdom in Women

A wise man does not chase. He attracts.
A wise man does not fall for beauty alone. He looks for substance.
A wise man does not allow lust to lead him into ruin.

History is full of men who conquered nations but lost everything because they could not control their desires.
Samson fell to Delilah.
Great rulers were undone by the wrong woman in their bed.

The downfall of many men was not war, not politics, not enemies, but a lack of discipline.
A fool wants the woman who excites his flesh.
A wise man wants the woman who strengthens his mind, his vision, his empire.
A fool is led by his urges.
A wise man is led by his discipline.
Choose wisely, or pay the price.

Do This At Once

- Ask yourself: Is the woman in my life making me better or distracting me from my mission?
- Stop chasing. Work on yourself, build your empire, and watch how the right women gravitate toward you.
- Master your discipline. If you cannot control your urges, you are not in control of your life.

Verse 5: Wisdom in Conflict

Not every battle is worth fighting.
A wise man knows when to stand his ground and when to walk away.
A fool fights every battle and wastes his energy on things that do not matter.
Pride has destroyed more men than bullets.

The world will test you. People will provoke you. Your enemies will try to pull you into a fight that you do not need to fight.
If you let your emotions control you, they will win before the fight even begins.
A wise man does not react.
He calculates.
He moves with strategy, not emotion.

When they insult you, when they challenge you, when they try
  to pull you down to their level, remember this:
A god does not respond to worms.

Do This At Once

- The next time someone disrespects you, pause. Do not react. Determine
- if they are worth your energy.
- Do not argue with fools. A fool's goal is to bring you down to his level.
- Save your battles for when they matter. A wise man fights only when
- there is something to gain.

Final Verse: The Responsibility of Wisdom

Wisdom is not just for you. It is to be passed down.

A fool hoards knowledge and keeps it to himself.
A wise man shares what he has learned, so that those who come
  after him do not make the same mistakes.

The world is filled with men who had potential but lacked
  wisdom.

Do not be one of them.

Do This At Once

- Teach one lesson you have learned to a younger man. Pass down your wisdom.

- Read one book this month that will sharpen your mind. Knowledge feeds wisdom.
- Move with precision, not emotion. Let every action be intentional.

Conclusion: Wisdom is Power

A man with knowledge is aware.

A man with wisdom is unstoppable.

Knowledge is what you know.

Wisdom is how you move.

If you seek power, if you seek mastery, if you seek to rise beyond the limits they set for you: Seek wisdom first.

The Infinite God Body moves with wisdom.

Book 3: Understanding

Amalgamation: Knowledge + Wisdom = Understanding

Knowledge is information, wisdom is using experience and your intellect to produce understanding. When you have true understanding then things become real. Things like the inner mind's eye, or the 3rd eye.

Verse 1: The Third Eye is the Mind, Not the Forehead

> They told you the third eye was mystical.
> That it was just some ancient symbol.
> That it was metaphorical.
> They lied.
>
> The third eye is real. It sits inside your skull.
> It is your pineal gland, a small organ in the center of your brain responsible for producing melatonin and serotonin, the hormones that regulate sleep, mood, and perception. More

importantly, it plays a role in producing DMT (dimethyltryptamine), the same compound that induces visions and heightened awareness.

This is why ancient Kemet's Eye of Horus is an exact representation of a cross-section of the brain. The ancients knew this was the gateway to higher consciousness.
But the world does not want you to see.

They fluoridate your water to calcify your pineal gland, keeping it dormant.
They bombard you with artificial light and stress to weaken your connection to reality.
They distract you with nonsense so you never focus on your own power.

Why? Because a blind mind is easy to control.
When your third eye is open, you see through deception.
You recognize patterns before they happen.
You are no longer a pawn in their game, you become the one who plays the board.

Do This At Once

- Get a water filter.
- Spend 10 minutes daily in complete darkness. The pineal gland is most active when free from artificial light.
- Eat foods rich in tryptophan and antioxidants. Bananas, walnuts, dark Chocolate, chlorella, salmon and spirulina support pineal function.
- Get sunlight first thing in the morning. Natural light sets your circadian rhythm and strengthens your third eye's ability to regulate reality.

Verse 2: Seeing the Unseen: Reading People and Situations

> Most people walk through life blind, not because they can't see, but because they never learned how.

There are three levels of sight:

i. First Vision **(physical)** – What your eyes perceive. This is the most basic level.

ii. Second Vision **(mental)** – The ability to read patterns, anticipate actions, and understand people's motives.

iii. Third Vision **(spiritual)** – The ability to see beyond the illusion, to recognize the hidden forces shaping the world.

> A wise man studies a person's body language, tone, and choice of words before he trusts them.
> A fool assumes everyone has good intentions.
> A wise man tests people before letting them close.
> Most people only use their physical sight, which is why they are easily
> fooled.

> They trust words instead of actions.
> They believe appearances over reality.
> They react instead of analyze.
> But when you master mental and spiritual sight, you will never be deceived again.

Do This At Once

- For the next 7 days, talk less and observe more. Watch how people behave when they don't think you're paying attention.
- Notice when people contradict themselves. Liars always slip up.
- Observe hand movements, eye contact, and breathing patterns. These reveal more than words ever could.

Verse 3: Beyond the Surface

Nothing in this world happens by accident.
Wars don't just start. They are orchestrated.
Economic crashes don't just happen. They are engineered.
The education system doesn't fail. It does exactly what it was designed
to do, keep people obedient and ignorant.

The world is not random.
It is a chessboard.
And if you don't understand the rules, you are a pawn.

They keep you distracted with gossip and entertainment while they:
Print trillions of dollars, devaluing your money
Buy up resources, owning everything while you rent
Rewrite laws, making sure the rich stay rich and the poor stay struggling
If you don't see it, you're not paying attention.

Do This At Once

- Track where your money goes. Understand how banks, taxes, and inflation work so you don't get robbed by the system.

- Turn off entertainment for a week. Watch how politicians and CEOs move instead. The real game isn't played on TV, it's played in boardrooms. Don't watch passively, try to understand their tactics, their strategies.
- Read about the Federal Reserve, central banking, and economic manipulation. Learn why debt is a tool of control.

Verse 4: Frequency is the Rate in Which Energy Vibrates.

Everything in existence has a frequency.
Your thoughts have a frequency.
Your emotions have a frequency.
The music you listen to, the words you speak, the food you eat, all of it influences your vibration.

This is not new information.
Nikola Tesla said: "If you want to find the secrets of the universe, think in terms of energy,
frequency, and vibration."

The well of wisdom that Nikola Tesla drank from was ancient Kemet.
The ancient Kemetic priests understood this. That's why their architecture, chants, and hieroglyphs were based on sacred geometry and harmonic resonance.
But today?

432 Hz music has been found to reduce stress and enhance clarity.
Mainstream music is deliberately tuned to 440 Hz, a dissonant frequency meant to keep people agitated and unbalanced. If your energy is low, if your thoughts are chaotic, if your emotions are
unstable, you are out of alignment with your natural frequency.

Do This At Once

- Listen to 432 Hz or 528 Hz frequencies daily. These recalibrate your nervous system.
- Stop watching toxic media. Everything you consume affects your frequency.
- Protect your energy. Stay away from low-vibrational people who drain your power.

Verse 5: The Art of War: Strategic Thinking in Daily Life

Sun Tzu said: "All war is deception."

You are always in a war. A war for your mind, your money, your health, your freedom.

The only question is: Are you fighting back, or are you being played?

A weak man reacts.
A wise man strategizes.

Your enemy wants you to be emotional.
Because emotional men are easy to control.

They will provoke you.
They will manipulate you.
They will make you act before you think, because the man who moves first without calculation always loses.

A god moves in silence, observes the battlefield, and strikes with precision.

Do This At Once

- Before making any decision, stop and ask: Who benefits from this?
- Never let someone control you through anger or fear. Master your emotions, and you master the game.
- Think two steps ahead. Never move without a reason.

Final Verse: Understanding is Power

Knowledge makes you aware.
Wisdom makes you act.
Understanding makes you unstoppable.

This is the level where you cannot be manipulated, deceived, or controlled.

They will call you crazy when you start seeing through the illusion.
They will say you are paranoid when you question the system.
They will say you are arrogant when you step into your power.

But remember,
A slave is never supposed to know he is a god.
You see it now. Act accordingly.

Book 4: Culture/Freedom

The Blueprint for Living as a God

Verse 1: Burn the Chains of a Dying Culture

The Western world is not your world.
It was built without you in mind.
The system they created was designed for your enslavement, not your success.

The laws, the customs, the economics, the media, all of it was shaped to keep you weak, distracted, and dependent.
Every structure that governs this world was built on plunder, deception, and mind control.

Understand this: Culture is the foundation of power.
A people without a sovereign culture will always be subjected to the
culture of their oppressors.

And what is the culture they gave you?
They gave you fast food instead of fuel.
They gave you entertainment instead of enlightenment.
They gave you distractions instead of dominion.
They gave you an economy designed to keep you poor, an education designed to keep you ignorant, and a morality designed to keep you submissive.

You were never meant to thrive in their system.
It is time to divorce yourself from it.
Burn the chains. Rewrite the laws. Build your own empire.

Do This At Once

- Eliminate all passive consumption of Western media. What you consume controls your perception of reality. Stop letting them shape your mind.
- Stop following their traditions blindly. Holidays, customs, institutions, ask yourself, Who does this benefit? If the answer is not you and your people, discard it.
- Declare your sovereignty. From this moment forward, you are not a subject of their world. You are a ruler of your own.

Verse 2: The Economy of a God – Own or Be Owned

The modern world has a new plantation. It's not a field, it's a paycheck.
They don't need chains anymore. They keep you in debt.
They don't need whips anymore. They keep you working check to check.
They don't need overseers anymore. They make you police yourself with the fear of losing a job.

A god is not a wage slave. A god does not beg for a paycheck.
A god owns land, resources, and businesses.
If another man controls your ability to eat, you are not free.
The true economy is ownership. If you do not own, you are owned.

The true currency is time. A god's time is never for sale.
The true investment is knowledge.
The rich buy assets.
The poor buy entertainment.

Do This At Once

Create an economic plan for total independence. What do you own?

What do you control? If the answer is nothing, your goal is to change that, immediately.

Eliminate all unnecessary spending. Every dollar spent on consumerism is a dollar you give to your masters.

Own land, assets, and businesses. The system is not built for you, so build your own.

Verse 3: Food is the First Weapon of War

They say, "You are what you eat." But they never told you that food is war.

If I wanted to destroy a people, I wouldn't need bombs, I'd just feed them poison.
They put high-fructose corn syrup in everything, because addiction is control.
They inject chemicals into livestock, because disease is profit.

They push processed food and sugar-heavy diets, because weakness is obedience.

Look at the modern Western diet, it is not food. It is a slow death.
A nation fed on junk becomes mentally sluggish, physically weak, and spiritually broken.

A god does not eat like a slave.
A god does not consume poison.
A god fuels himself for war, not for weakness.

Do This At Once

- Purge your kitchen of ALL processed foods. If it has ingredients you can't pronounce, it doesn't belong in your body.
- Eat for function, not pleasure. A king does not feast for entertainment.
- Eat for power.
- Fast regularly. If you cannot control your hunger, you cannot control your
- mind.

Verse 4: The Death of the Nuclear Family – Rebuilding the Throne

In ancient cultures, the family was the strongest unit of power.
The father was the king. The mother was the queen. The children were future warriors and rulers.

The Western system knew this, so they destroyed it.
They feminized men to remove strong leadership.
They masculinized women to break the natural balance.

They created welfare systems that incentivized fatherless homes.
They pushed sexual liberation to turn relationships into transactions.
They broke the throne, because a people without strong families are easier to rule.

It is time to restore order.

Do This At Once

- Men: Become rulers of your household.
- Lead with wisdom, strength, and discipline.
- Women: Embrace your divine feminine power.
- The greatest empires were built on the backs of strong women who nurtured kings.
- Build families, not flings. A strong bloodline is an empire.

Verse 5: The Culture of War – Prepare for Battle Daily

The world is at war.
The economy is at war.
Your mind is at war.
Your legacy is at war.

And yet, you were taught to live as if peace was the default condition of life.
This was the greatest lie ever told.

Every day, the weak are conquered.
Every day, the strong take what they want.
Every day, those who are unprepared become prey.
A god does not live in peace. He lives in readiness.

Do This At Once

- Train your body daily.
- Weakness invites oppression.
- Strength commands respect.
- Master a combat skill.
- If you cannot protect yourself and your family, you are already conquered.
- Move strategically.
- Think tactically.
- Stop reacting to life.
- Start planning your next five moves in advance.

Verse 6: The Cultural Renaissance – The Age of Gods

We are at the beginning of a new cycle.

The age of submission is over.
The age of gods has begun.
But no revolution is won without culture.
A people who do not have their own culture will always be slaves to another.

It is time to restore the codes of our ancestors and create a new order:
Honor over profit.
Strength over comfort.
Discipline over indulgence.
Creation over consumption.
Sovereignty over submission.

We are the architects of a new civilization.
And this time, we are the rulers.

Mike Rashid King

Final Verse: Culture is the Throne of Power

No empire has ever stood without a sovereign culture.

The Romans had theirs.
The Greeks had theirs.
The British had theirs.

What do you have?
If you are adopting their culture, you are living under their rule.
If you want power, if you want legacy, if you want to break the cycle of subjugation, there is only one option:

Destroy the system that made you weak.
Reclaim the knowledge that made you strong.
Live as a god. Move as a god. Build as a god.

The Infinite God Body is awake.

Book 5: Power & Refinement

The Force to Build, Sustain, and Elevate

In Supreme Mathematics, five represents Power, the raw force that shapes realities, topples empires, and ignites change. Yet power alone is fleeting, a spark that burns out without direction. Refinement is its mastery, the discipline that turns a wildfire into a laser, a brute into a god. The Infinite God Body wields power not to dominate, but to create, sustain, and elevate. This is the path of the Black Overman, forged in Kemet's wisdom, tempered by the Moors' precision, and guided by the Most Honorable Elijah Muhammad's vision. Power without refinement is chaos; power with refinement is divinity. Through these verses, you will learn to harness your strength, sharpen your focus, and build legacies that outlast time. The cipher of five demands mastery, claim it now.

Verse 1: Power Without Refinement is a Short-Lived Kingdom

> Power alone is a brute force. It seizes but does not sustain, conquers but does not govern, wins battles but does not win

history. A strong man can take over a village, but only a refined man can build a civilization. Consider the warrior who swings wildly, only to tire and fall, or the king who rules by fear, only to be overthrown. In Mali, Mansa Musa's power was vast, but his refinement, building universities and trade networks, made his empire eternal. The world is littered with men who grasped power but lacked the precision to hold it. A boxer with strength but no technique is knocked out; a mogul with wealth but no strategy goes bankrupt. Raw power is a spark; refinement is the forge that shapes it into a blade. Without refinement, your kingdom is temporary, your throne destined to crumble.

Do This At Once

- Ask yourself: Am I chasing power, or refining it into something greater? Write one area where your power lacks precision.
- Study a historical ruler (e.g., Mansa Musa, Marcus Garvey) for 30 minutes, note how they refined their power.
- Commit to one daily action to sharpen a skill, making your power surgical.

Verse 2: Refinement is Mastery Over Power

The highest form of power is mastery, where every move is deliberate, every action precise. An unrefined warrior swings a sword wildly; a refined warrior kills with a single stroke. An unrefined speaker talks to be heard; a refined speaker says little but commands kings. In Kemet, the architects of the pyramids aligned stones with cosmic precision, reflecting the divine order. Refinement turns power into art, presence into a weapon, action into strategy. The Moors built Córdoba's grandeur not through chaos, but through disciplined intellect. A fool believes power is doing more; a god knows power is doing less, but making every move count. Master your craft, your mind, your spirit, let no motion be wasted.

Do This At Once

- Practice stillness for 5 minutes daily, control your breath, focus your mind, eliminate distractions.
- Study a precision-based master (e.g., samurai, chess grandmaster) for 1 hour, emulate their focus.
- Cut one unnecessary action from your day (e.g., mindless scrolling), redirect that energy to a refined goal.

Verse 3: The Power of Restraint - A Master Strikes Only When Necessary

A weak man acts on impulse; a refined man acts on calculation. The loudest man in the room is never the most powerful, he seeks validation, not victory. The first to attack in anger often falls first. Restraint is not weakness; it is the highest form of control. The Nation of Islam's discipline under Elijah Muhammad turned rage into revolution, not riots. A fool swings at every punch; a master waits for the perfect moment and ends the fight with one strike. Restraint conserves your power, making you untouchable. They will provoke you, insult you, tempt you, but a god does not respond to worms. Move only when the time is right, and let your strike be final.

Do This At Once

- The next time you feel provoked, pause for 10 seconds, observe, don't react. Write what you learned.
- Practice silence for one day, speak only when necessary, noting how restraint amplifies your presence.
- Plan one strategic response to a challenge this week, act only when it maximizes impact.

Verse 4: Refinement is the Art of Building, Not Just Destroying

A fool destroys; a god creates. A fool conquers land but lets it waste; a god builds an empire that lasts generations. A fool tears down enemies and calls it victory; a god turns enemies into assets, making his power unshakable. In Timbuktu, scholars built libraries that outshone Europe's Dark Ages, not through war but through refined knowledge. Your power must create, businesses, families, philosophies. What will your name mean when you're gone? A fleeting spark, or a beacon through time? Refinement ensures your creations endure, your legacy immortal.

Do This At Once

- Start one creative project today (e.g., a journal, a business idea), make it tangible by nightfall.
- Mentor someone, turning their potential into an asset for your shared vision.
- Write a 5-year plan for your legacy, what will you build that cannot be erased?

Verse 5: Refinement Through Adversity

Power is forged in the crucible of struggle; refinement is honed in adversity. Every chain, every lash, every lie your ancestors endured was a fire that tempered their spirit. Malcolm X was not born a leader, he was refined in prison, his pain sharpening his vision. Adversity is not your enemy; it is your teacher. The world will test you with loss, betrayal, and oppression. A fool crumbles; a god emerges stronger. Each challenge is a chance to refine your power, to strip away weakness, to align with the divine order. Embrace struggle as the anvil that shapes your Infinite God Body.

Do This At Once

- Identify one current struggle, write how it can refine your character or skills.
- Study a figure who overcame adversity (e.g., Malcolm X, Harriet Tubman) for 30 minutes, apply one lesson.
- Face one fear this week, act despite discomfort to hone your resilience.

Final Verse: Power Without Refinement is Just a Temporary Throne

Power without refinement is a muscle without coordination, strong but clumsy, capable of breaking but not building. A king with power but no refinement is a future fallen king; a fighter with strength but no technique is a future defeated warrior. Raw power makes a tyrant; refined power makes a god. Refine yourself daily, master your thoughts, hone your actions, build with purpose. In Kemet, the Eye of Horus saw truth through chaos; your refined power must see the same. The Infinite God Body is awake, wield it with precision, and your throne will stand eternal.

Daily Practice for the God Body

For five days, refine your power through disciplined focus. Each morning, spend 5 minutes visualizing a goal executed with flawless precision. During the day, eliminate one impulsive action (e.g., reacting to provocation, wasting time). At night, journal one way you moved with restraint or creation. By day five, your power will feel sharper, your presence more commanding, your purpose clearer.

Conclusion: The Refined God Builds Forever

Power is your birthright; refinement is your crown. Together, they make you unstoppable, a creator, a sustainer, a divine force. The world fears your refined power, for it cannot be chained or dimmed. Move with the precision of the Moors, the vision of Mansa Musa, the discipline of Elijah Muhammad. Build empires, not ruins. Elevate humanity, not yourself alone. The Infinite God Body is refined, radiant, and eternal. Claim your throne, and let your creations echo through the ages.

Book 6: Equality

The Equilibrium of Knowledge, Wisdom, and Understanding

In Supreme Mathematics, six represents Equality – the state of perfect balance. It means being equal in all aspects, grounded in knowledge, wisdom, and understanding. The ancients revered the number 6 as a symbol of harmony; it is the first perfect number, because $1 + 2 + 3$ equals 6. When knowledge, wisdom, and understanding unite, they produce a power greater than the sum of their parts, a state of equilibrium where nothing is lacking. But equality is not merely a number; it is a principle of life. It is the justice that balances the scales of existence, the harmony between the divine and the earthly.

Yet six is also the number of limitations. It represents the boundary of the physical, the point where many fall prey to complacency. Six is one step short of seven – God – which means if you stop at equality without striving further, you risk stagnation.

. . .

The devil operates in this realm of limitation, convincing you that six is all there is. He wants you satisfied with mere survival, content with the scraps of false equality that society throws at your feet. He fears what happens when you realize there is more, that beyond the balance of six lies the divine power of seven. To master equality, you must understand its dual nature: the balance that empowers, and the limitation that must be overcome.

Verse 1: The Mathematics of Balance

> Equality is the great equation of life. Knowledge + Wisdom + Understanding = Equality. This is not just arithmetic; it is a law of growth. Without all three, you will always be incomplete. A man with knowledge and wisdom but no understanding is out of balance, he may know and do, but not grasp why. A man with wisdom and understanding but no true knowledge is misguided, he moves and feels, but on a foundation of sand. To stand firm as a god, you need all three pillars

strong and equal.

> They hid this truth from you.
> They taught you fragments, never the whole.

> Schools gave you knowledge, but not wisdom.
> Religions gave you wisdom in parables, but discouraged personal understanding.
> They fear the day you combine all three.

> Because a man who knows, who acts on what he knows wisely, and who understands the deeper meaning, that man cannot be controlled.

> He is equal to any challenge, balanced in mind, body, and spirit. When you achieve this

internal equality, you become calm, unshakable. The world cannot knock a balanced man down; every hit is absorbed and countered with Precision.

Do This At Once

- Audit your mind: List something you know (knowledge), how you have applied it (wisdom), and what it taught you about life (understanding). Identify any of the three that you are neglecting, and commit to strengthening it.
- Practice balance in action. Today, for every hour you spend training your body, spend an hour feeding your mind. For every moment of taking in knowledge, spend a moment in reflection to gain understanding.
- Equalize your respect: Treat someone as an equal today.
- Speak to the janitor, the clerk, or the stranger with the same espect you would give a king. Observe how this balance of respect empowers you both.

Mike Rashid King

Verse 2: The Devil's Domain – False Equality

They promised you "all men are created equal," while chaining your ancestors to the bottom of ships.

They preached equality in their constitutions and prayers, even as they drew color lines and built systems of injustice. The devil is a master of illusions: he uses the word equality to placate you, to make you think balance has been achieved – all while the scales are tipped outrageously in his favor.

This is false equality, a poisoned lie. It's the offer of a seat at a rigged table.

Understand this: the devil's equality is limitation. It's a ceiling over your head, a chain on your ankle, a deal that says "stay in your place, and we will treat you almost as equal." They want you to celebrate token victories while real power stays in their hands. They want you to be content with crumbs while they feast. This is the equality of the oppressor: a balance where he sits above and you below, and calls it justice. Reject it completely.

A god does not beg for equality from his enemies. A god takes his equality by rising to his own power. You were not created to be "equal enough" you were born to break any limit they set for you, to shatter every ceiling imposed on you by devils in disguise.

Do This At Once

- Shatter a ceiling: Identify one area in your life where you've accepted less than you deserve. It could be at work, in society, or in a relationship. Today, decide to break that limitation – take one action to claim the respect or opportunity you are due.

- Seize your rights: Stop expecting your oppressor to hand you equality. Shift your mindset to seize it. If there is a right or resource you've been denied, plan how to obtain it through your own means or with your community's support, not through begging.
- Expose a false balance: Think of a situation that seems "fair" on the surface but is unfair underneath (a law, a policy, a double standard). Speak out about it or educate someone on why it's unjust. Refuse to silently accept false equality.

Verse 3: Woman – The Other Half of Equality

In the mathematics of life, woman is a powerful factor. The union of man and woman is meant to be an equation of balance, two beings adding to each other's strength. But the wrong woman can throw your entire equation off.

Many great men have been destroyed by lust, distraction, or a partnership that pulled them away from their purpose. The scriptures tell of Samson brought low by Delilah, of Adam led astray by Eve's temptation. These are not tales to blame womanhood – they are
warnings to choose wisely and maintain balance.

A fool chases a woman's body and neglects his destiny.
A wise man wants the woman who strengthens his mind, his vision, his empire.

In Supreme Mathematics, equality also means being equal in knowledge, man and woman elevating each other mentally and spiritually. If your queen does not know what you know, teach her. If she cannot support the mission, examine if she is meant to walk this path with you.

A god and earth (woman) together form a powerful cipher of life, but only if both sides are balanced. Do not let desire chain you to a partner who keeps you earth-bound. The right woman will help you fly; the wrong woman will weigh you down into limitation.

Do This At Once

- Assess your union: Evaluate the primary relationship in your life. Ask yourself if your partner (or the person you pursue) truly makes you better in knowledge, wisdom, and understanding.
- Have an honest conversation with them about growth and purpose, or make the hard choice to distance yourself if they consistently pull you off your path.
- Master your urges: Go 7 days without indulging in sexual vice or pornography. Prove to yourself that you control your desires rather than being controlled by them.
- Channel that energy into your goals and self-mastery.
- Build together: If you have a queen who stands by you, elevate her. Share a book or lesson that has enlightened you, and learn something from her in return. Build each other up so that you move in equal stride toward your destiny.

Verse 4: The Scales of Justice on the Path to Godhood

> Equality is not only personal, it is the law by which gods rule. Every great civilization had at its core a concept of divine justice. In Kemet, the goddess Ma'at weighed the hearts of men against a feather to judge their souls, a perfect balance between truth and righteousness.
>
> King Solomon, famed for wisdom, once invoked a harsh test (splitting a child) to reveal the true mother, demonstrating that justice unveils truth.

Understand that to be a god, you must wield power with fairness and mercy. Without equality, power turns to tyranny. Without justice, a king becomes a monster.

A true god seeks to equalize, to lift the oppressed, to bring balance where there is chaos. Equality is the sword and the scale of the enlightened ruler. It cuts down injustice and measures all with the same standard

If you wear the crown, you cannot play favorites with truth. You cannot be swayed by bribes, lust, or fear. You must be balanced in judgment, as impartial as that ancient scale of Ma'at. This is the responsibility that comes with godhood: to create order, harmony, and equality in your domain. Anything less, and you are not a god, but a fraud sitting on a brittle throne.

Do This At Once

- Be a fair judge: The next time you are in a position to decide an outcome that affects others, pause and remove your personal biases. Weigh the facts as if the people involved were strangers.
- Make the choice that upholds fairness, even if it's difficult.
- Right a wrong: Find one wrong in your environment that you have the power to set right – an unfair rule, a person being mistreated or neglected – and intervene to balance the scales. Even a small act of justice is a step toward godliness.
- Weigh your heart: Each night, reflect on your actions. Mentally weigh your heart against the feather of truth. Where were you fair and where did you falter? Resolve to correct any imbalance the next day, keeping yourself true and just.

The Divine Quintessence

Final Verse: Beyond the Six – Ascending to Divinity

> Equality achieved is not the end; it is the bridge to your highest self.
> When you have balanced knowledge, wisdom, and understanding in yourself and in how you deal with the world, you stand at the gateway of seven.

> The sixth step makes you a man restored to his full potential, but the seventh makes you God. The devil cannot survive in the realm of seven, for there all illusion is destroyed. At seven, there is only godhood– supreme intelligence and righteousness in action.

> Do not stop at equality and think the journey is complete.
> Use it as your launching pad.

> The moment of perfect balance is the moment right before ascension. Like the stillness at the top of a great breath before you exhale power, equality is that stillness – poised, ready to become something greater. Now step into the realm of God.

> Let the harmony you've built carry you upward to create, to lead, to define justice and truth on Earth.
> The Infinite God Body within you demands this elevation.

Conclusion: Equality is the Great Balance

Equality is the fulcrum upon which your evolution pivots. It is the state of being centered, unshakeable in truth. It is your harmony with all, ensuring your rise lifts others as well.

. . .

With equality, you stand firm against any storm. Balanced in knowledge, wisdom, and understanding, you cannot be deceived or divided.

This is why they fear a balanced

Black man, he is free, he is powerful, and he is divine. But remember: equality must be maintained and then surpassed.

Balance is not a one-time achievement but a living practice. Continually check yourself: mind and heart, strength and compassion, ambition and humility – all in balance. In doing so, you keep your foundation strong.

And on that foundation, you rise to godhood.

The path to seven is open. Step forward, armed with the power of six in perfect balance. For when you move in equality, nothing can shake the Infinite God Body within you.

Book 7: God/Allah

The Divine Essence Realized

In Supreme Mathematics, Seven symbolizes God/Allah, the supreme consciousness within man, the divine spark that transcends physical limitation and ignites infinite potential. Godhood is not an external deity to beg from, nor an unreachable force beyond the stars. It is the essence already within you, pulsing through your blood, drawn from Kemet's wisdom and the Supreme Wisdom of the Most Honorable Elijah Muhammad. To claim godhood is to awaken the Infinite God Body, to stand as a creator, a righteous force, a master of self and reality. This is not blasphemy but truth: you are the god you've been waiting for. The world fears this awakening, for a god bows to no chains, answers to no oppressor, and builds empires from the ashes of lies. Through these verses, you will learn to embody this divine essence, to move with supreme intelligence, righteousness, and creative power. The cipher of seven is your birthright, step into it now.

Verse 1: The Divine Essence Realized

God/Allah is not a mystery locked in the heavens; it is the living fire within your soul. The number seven in Supreme Mathematics represents the completion of a cycle, the moment when knowledge, wisdom, and understanding fuse into divine consciousness. This is the spark that shaped the cosmos, the same force that flows through your veins. The Most Honorable Elijah Muhammad taught that God appeared in the Person of Master Fard Muhammad, not to rule over us, but to reveal our own divinity. Look in the mirror: you are not separate from this power. Every thought you hold, every action you take, is a divine act when aligned with truth. Yet, this realization demands responsibility. A god does not drift through life; a god creates with purpose, lives with righteousness, and uplifts humanity. The world fears this truth, for a slave is never meant to know he is a god. They silenced Yeshua for declaring, "Ye are gods" (Psalm 82:6), and they will try to silence you. But their fear cannot dim your light. Awaken now, Black god, and let your essence reshape reality.

Do This At Once

- Meditate for 10 minutes daily, visualizing your inner spark as a radiant light connecting you to the universe.
- Write a letter to your future self, declaring how you will embody godhood in one year.
- Teach one person about the divine within them, sparking their awakening.

Verse 2: Supreme Intelligence

Godhood is supreme intelligence, the ability to see through illusions, discern truth from deception, and calculate your movements with precision. A god does not react; a god responds strategically. Your mind is a cosmos, sharper than any blade, capable of unraveling the systems that bind you. In Kemet, the priests of Ra harnessed intellect to map the stars; today, you must harness yours to map your destiny. The Nation of Islam's Supreme Wisdom teaches that knowledge is the foundation, but intelligence is its mastery. Study the chessboard of life, every move by your oppressors, every lie in their media, every law that chains you. See the patterns, anticipate their plays, and counter with divine clarity. A god's intellect is eternal, always learning, always refining. To be less is to betray your essence.

Do This At Once

- Read one book per week on a subject you know little about, stretching your intellect beyond comfort.
- Observe a situation deeply, seeking the hidden mechanics behind it. Write down three insights you uncover.
- Challenge one lie you encounter today, whether in conversation or media, with a question that exposes its weakness.

Verse 3: Embodying Righteousness

God is not merely power; God is righteous power. A tyrant wields strength without principle, but a god wields strength with justice. Righteousness is your compass, guiding every decision, every word, every act. The scales of Ma'at in Kemet weighed the heart against truth; your heart must weigh the same. Stand against injustice, even when it costs you. Speak truth, even when it isolates you. The Most Honorable Elijah Muhammad built a nation on righteousness, refusing to bow to oppression. You must do the same. A god does not compromise his principles for comfort, popularity, or safety. Your integrity is your crown, wear it unbowed.

Do This At Once

- Identify one injustice in your environment, speak out against it, intervene boldly, correct it actively.
- Hold yourself accountable: never break your word, never betray trust. Write a pledge to uphold your integrity.
- Mentor a younger person, teaching them to stand firm in righteousness.

Verse 4: God as the Creator

You are a builder by divine nature. Creation is the language of gods, art, business, empires, culture, wisdom. A god does not complain about circumstances; he creates new ones. In Mali, Mansa Musa built wealth and knowledge that dazzled the world; you must build legacies that echo through time. Your creations are proof of your divinity, tangible evidence that God dwells within you. Whether you write a book, start a movement, or raise a family, every act of creation is a defiance of oppression. The world waits for your mark, leave it boldly.

Do This At Once

- Create something meaningful today, a poem, a business plan, a community project. Act now, not tomorrow.
- Share your creation with one person, inspiring them to build their own.
- Outline your legacy: what will your name mean in 100 years? Take one step toward it now.

The Divine Quintessence

Verse 5: Mastering Self, Mastering Reality

Godhood demands supreme discipline. A god is not swayed by urges, impulses, or distractions. Your body, mind, and emotions must serve you, not enslave you. The Moors mastered sciences and governance through discipline; you must master yourself through the same. Control your thoughts, for they shape your reality. Control your body, for it is your temple. Control your spirit, for it is your connection to the infinite. Only when you master self can you master the world. Discipline is your daily offering to your godhood.

Do This At Once

- Fast for one day this week, proving your dominance over physical desires.
- Discipline your emotions: when anger or fear arises, pause, breathe, and respond with calm clarity.
- Create a daily schedule that prioritizes your growth, follow it without excuse.

Verse 6: God as Unity

Godhood is not solitary; it is unity. To see the divine in yourself is to see it in others. The Nation of Islam teaches that every Black man is a god, and every Black woman an earth, together, you form a cipher of creation. This unity extends beyond race, for the Infinite God Body is the spark in all who seek truth. Build communities, not divisions. Lift your brothers and sisters, not your ego. The pyramids of Kemet were built by collective will; your empire must be built the same. A god who stands alone is mighty, but a god who unites is unstoppable.

Do This At Once

- Organize a study group to discuss divine principles with your community.
- Perform one act of selfless service today, help someone without expecting reward.
- Write a vision for a unified community project and share it with three people.

Verse 7: The God Cipher

Seven is a cipher, a full circle of godly wisdom. You began with knowledge, moved through wisdom, understanding, culture, power, and equality. Now, in godhood, the cipher completes. You are infinitely greater than before, a born-again god fortified in truth. This is not the end but a new beginning. Teach this path to others, for in teaching, you deepen your mastery. The world will test your godhood, temptation, doubt, oppression. Welcome these as chances to prove your divine nature. Your power shines brightest in struggle, your divinity clearest in defiance.

Do This At Once

- Mentor someone younger, passing down one lesson from your journey.
- Reflect weekly on your growth: where have you risen, where must you evolve?

- Declare your godhood daily: stand before a mirror and say, "I am God/Allah, creator of my reality."

Final Verse: Eternal Awakening

Godhood is not static; it is eternal awakening. Every day, reaffirm your divinity, reassert your mastery, recommit to elevating self and others. The world will challenge you daily, temptation, doubt, oppression. Embrace these tests as forges for your divine steel. Your power is proven not in comfort, but in struggle. Your divinity shines brightest when challenged. Stand tall, Black god. Stand firm, divine being. The Infinite God Body within you is fully awake, and in your awakening, all humanity sees the path to liberation.

Daily Practice for the God Body

For seven days, embody your godhood through disciplined action. Each morning, meditate for 5 minutes, affirming, "I am the divine spark, creator of my world." During the day, perform one righteous act, correct an injustice, share wisdom, or build something meaningful. At night, journal one way you manifested your divinity. By day seven, you will feel the Infinite God Body alive within you, unshakable and radiant.

Conclusion: You Are the God You've Been Waiting For

No longer seek salvation in external forces. The power you seek resides in your reflection. Godhood is your birthright, your true nature. Claim it fully. Walk boldly as the god you are, a living embodiment of supreme wisdom, righteousness, and creative power. In your godhood, the world finds its salvation. The Infinite God Body is awake. You are the divine made manifest.

Book 8: Build and Destroy

The Cycle of Creation and Elimination

In Supreme Mathematics, Eight represents Build and Destroy, the eternal rhythm of creation and elimination that drives divine evolution. Life is a cycle of growth and pruning, innovation and eradication, construction and demolition. To ascend to true godhood, you must master both forces. Building without destroying stagnation breeds decay; destroying without purposeful building leads to ruin. The Infinite God Body is a divine architect, crafting empires from the ashes of oppression, and a relentless warrior, tearing down systems that chain the soul. From Kemet's pyramids to Timbuktu's libraries, our ancestors built legacies that endure; from the Moors' conquests to Elijah Muhammad's revolution, they destroyed what hindered truth. Through these verses, you will learn to create with vision and eliminate with precision, forging a throne that stands eternal. The cipher of eight is your mandate—build boldly, destroy decisively.

Verse 1: The Divine Architect

You were not born to survive, you were born to build. Civilization rose from gods who shaped chaos into greatness, from the Nile's stone pyramids to Mali's golden markets. They saw the world not as it was, but as it could be. In Timbuktu, scholars built Sankore University, a beacon of knowledge that outshone Europe's Dark Ages. But no structure rises on rotten foundations. To build anew, you must first destroy, false beliefs, toxic habits, weak alliances. The Most Honorable Elijah Muhammad built a nation by tearing down the slave mind, replacing it with divine truth. You are the architect of your reality. Design with purpose, clear the debris, and lay a foundation that withstands time.

Do This At Once

- Identify one limiting belief holding you back, write it down, burn it, declare it destroyed.
- Start one project today (e.g., a business plan, artwork), act now to bring your vision to life.
- Study Timbuktu's scholars for 30 minutes, note one way they built enduring knowledge.

Verse 2: Destroy the Illusions

Society chains you with illusions, lies masquerading as truth. Eurocentric systems, media propaganda, and consumerist traps are invisible shackles. They tell you happiness lies in possessions, validation, comfort. But godhood lies in purpose, discipline, struggle. In Kemet, the Eye of Horus pierced illusions to see divine order; you must do the same. Destroy the lie that you are small, that your power is limited, that their world is your world. The Papal Bulls of the 15th century declared you less than human, tear that lie apart. Clear your mind of their narratives, and build your truth on the foundation of Supreme Wisdom.

Do This At Once

- Identify one societal lie you've accepted (e.g., materialism equals success), write it, tear it up, reject it forever.
- Challenge one false narrative publicly today, speak truth in a conversation or post.
- Replace one hour of media consumption with studying Supreme Wisdom or Afrocentric history.

Verse 3: Eliminate the Weakness Within

No empire falls without internal weakness. A god hunts his flaws, laziness, doubt, impulsiveness, and destroys them mercilessly. Comfort zones breed mediocrity; they must be demolished. Malcolm X destroyed his criminal past in prison, refining himself into a divine force. Your weaknesses are not your identity; they are obstacles to your godhood. The Nation of Islam's discipline turned broken men into gods through relentless self-scrutiny. Identify what holds you back, fear, procrastination, anger, and eradicate it. This destruction makes room for strength, wisdom, and divinity.

Do This At Once

- Write one habit that weakens you (e.g., procrastination), commit to eliminating it this week.
- Replace that habit with a strengthening action (e.g., daily planning for discipline).
- Reflect nightly: what weakness did I destroy today? Journal your progress.

Verse 4: Builders or Parasites

Humanity splits into two: builders who create and parasites who consume. A parasite destroys without building, takes without giving, feeds on others' work. Gods build civilizations; parasites drain them. In Mali, Mansa Musa built wealth and culture, not for himself, but for generations. A god contributes more than he takes, creates more than he consumes. Your circle defines your kingdom, surround yourself with builders who elevate, not parasites who deplete. Audit your life: are you a creator or a taker? Build with purpose, or you risk becoming the parasite you despise.

Do This At Once

- Audit your circle, list five people you spend time with. Remove one parasite who drains you.
- Collaborate with a builder, start a project with someone who pushes you to grow.
- Create one tangible contribution today (e.g., teach a skill, share wisdom), prove you're a builder.

Verse 5: The Discipline of Destruction

Destruction is not chaos, it is surgical precision. A surgeon removes diseased tissue to save the patient; a god removes what hinders growth. The Moors destroyed outdated systems in Al-Andalus, building a multicultural empire in their place. This disciplined destruction clears space for new life, ideas, relationships, realities. End toxic connections, unproductive routines, limiting mindsets. The Nation of Islam destroyed the slave mentality to build a divine nation.

Prune your reality with intent, and watch your empire rise from the cleared ground.

Do This At Once

- Eliminate one draining obligation today (e.g., a toxic relationship, time-wasting habit).
- Replace it with a growth-enhancing action (e.g., study, exercise, spiritual practice).
- Write a plan to strategically destroy one obstacle this month—execute it with precision.

Verse 6: Legacy Building

A god does not live for today; he builds for eternity. Your purpose transcends personal gain, it is a testimony for generations. In Kemet, the pyramids stand as proof of divine legacy; your creations must do the same. Destroy short-term thinking, trivial distractions, fleeting pleasures. Build institutions, wealth, wisdom that outlive you. Marcus Garvey built the UNIA to uplift a race; your legacy must uplift humanity. What will your name mean in a century? Act now to ensure it echoes through time.

Do This At Once

- Outline your legacy, write what you want to leave behind in 100 years.
- Take one action toward it today (e.g., invest in education, mentor someone).
- Study a legacy-builder (e.g., Garvey, Muhammad) for 30 minutes, apply one principle.

Verse 7: Destroying Systemic Barriers

The systems of oppression, economic, educational, judicial, are walls built to confine your godhood. Destroy them not with rage, but with strategy. The Nation of Islam built schools and businesses to break dependence on Eurocentric systems. You must do the same. Create your own economy, educate your own mind, define your own justice. Every dollar spent in their system strengthens their walls; every dollar invested in your community tears them down. Systemic destruction is not vengeance, it is liberation, clearing the path for divine creation.

Do This At Once

- Identify one systemic barrier you face (e.g., economic dependence), write a plan to bypass it.
- Support a Black-owned business or community initiative this week, invest in liberation.
- Educate one person about a systemic lie (e.g., biased education), spread truth.

Verse 8: Collective Building

A god builds alone, but a pantheon builds together. The Infinite God Body is not solitary, it is the collective power of gods and earths united. In Kemet, communities raised pyramids; in Mali, griots wove collective wisdom. The Nine Ministries of the Nation of Islam show that a nation rises when all build together, agriculture, education, defense, culture. Your legacy is stronger when shared. Unite with builders, create systems, uplift your people. A single god is mighty; a unified cipher is unstoppable.

Do This At Once

- Organize a community project (e.g., study group, garden), start it this week.
- Mentor a group of three people, teaching them to build together.
- Write a vision for a collective legacy, share it with your circle.

Final Verse: The Eternal Cycle of Elevation

> Build and Destroy is the breath of gods, eternal, rhythmic, alive. To stagnate is death; to build and prune is life. The Infinite God Body moves in constant growth, destroying mediocrity to build mastery, erasing weakness to forge strength. In Kemet, the phoenix rose from ashes; you must rise the same. Accept no limits, settle for no half-measures. Build with the vision of Mansa Musa, destroy with the precision of the Moors. Your existence is this rhythm, create with purpose, eliminate with clarity. The world awaits your empire.

Daily Practice for the God Body

For eight weeks, embody the cycle of Build and Destroy. Each week, focus on one verse's principle. Week 1: Destroy a limiting belief, build a new vision. Week 2: Eliminate a media illusion, study truth. Week 3: Eradicate a personal weakness, strengthen a skill. Week 4: Remove a parasite, collaborate with a builder. Week 5: End a draining habit, start a growth practice. Week 6: Plan a legacy, take one step. Week 7: Bypass a systemic barrier, invest in community. Week 8: Organize a collective project, unite builders. Each day, spend 5 minutes visualizing your empire rising from cleared ground. Journal nightly: what did I destroy, what did I build? By week eight, your Infinite God Body will pulse with creative and destructive power.

Conclusion: Build Your Throne from the Ruins

Mastery of Build and Destroy is the key to immortal godhood. Build consciously, destroy deliberately, and your empire will stand eternal. The ruins of oppression are your raw material; the wisdom of your ancestors is your blueprint. Move now, build greatness, destroy obstacles, claim your throne. The Infinite God Body is awake, a divine force of creation and elimination. Let your legacy be the proof, your empire the testament.

Book 9: Born

The Power of 9 in the Cycle of Rebirth

We have arrived at the ninth and final stage of our journey through Infinite God Body. In the language of Supreme Mathematics, the number 9 represents Born, the point of complete realization, where all prior building blocks culminate in the birth of a new reality. Just as a child emerges after nine months in the womb, the spiritual significance of nine is that of completion and rebirth. It is the stage at which the seed of knowledge planted in darkness breaks through into the light, fully formed and ready to manifest. In this culminating chapter, we explore why 9 is the number of divine birth and completion, and how embracing its power can trigger our own transformation.

Nine is not merely the end of a cycle; it is the dawn of a new existence. In mathematics, it is the highest single digit, after 9 we return to 0, signaling a fresh start at a higher octave. Spiritually, the journey from 1 (Knowledge) through 8 (Build/Destroy) finds its fulfillment in 9 (Born), meaning that all the understanding and growth attained must now be born in reality. This chapter stands as the capstone of Infinite God Body, synthesizing all prior lessons into a profound call to rebirth. As you read, feel the weight of this knowledge, let it move you to action

and prepare you to embrace your own divine rebirth. The power of 9 is the power to finish what was started and step forth anew.

NINE: THE NUMBER OF DIVINE BIRTH AND COMPLETION

Nine is the number of completion. It signifies the end of a cycle and the beginning of life in a new form. The Honorable Elijah Muhammad taught that the number 9 is directly connected to the divine completion of Creation, notably the nine months it takes for a woman to carry and give birth to a child . This is not coincidence but providence: just as it requires nine months for the physical body of a baby to be perfectly formed in the womb, so too does the spirit follow cycles of development that culminates in a new birth. When something (an idea, a project, a phase of life) reaches its ninth stage, it is ready to be born into reality, fully matured and complete. Nine is the fruition of all prior effort, the flower that blooms after the roots have done their unseen work.

In the teachings of Supreme Mathematics, 9, Born means to bring into existence that did not exist before. It is both a physical birth and a mental/spiritual birth. Physically, it is the moment a child draws its first breath. Mentally, it is the moment enlightenment manifests, when the

knowledge and wisdom we've cultivated finally materialize as understanding, action, and creation. Think of the previous stages (Knowledge, Wisdom, Understanding, etc.) as trimesters of pregnancy for the mind and soul. By the time we reach the ninth, everything is in place; the vision conceived in Knowledge is now ready to live. Completion in this sense is not an end, but a grand moment of transition, the cocoon opens and the new being emerges. Nine, the number of divine birth, signals that we have arrived at a threshold.

. . .

Crossing it, we are born again in consciousness, prepared to start a new cycle on a higher plane.

The Universal Order of 9 – The Solar System and Universal Balance

What is true in the microcosm of human life is reflected in the macrocosm of the heavens. The universe itself testifies to the power of 9. Consider our solar system: nine planets orbit around one sun in perfect balance and order, according to the teachings of the Honorable Elijah Muhammad. This celestial arrangement is a divine signpost, a grand model of completion and harmony. Each of the 9 planets completes its rotation around the sun, contributing to the cosmic family.

Together they form a unified system, just as all aspects of our being must come together around the light of truth. Nine signifies universal balance: the planets move in ordained paths, just as our lives find alignment when centered on divine purpose.

The sun, with its tremendous gravitational pull, holds the nine planets in orbit, providing light and life. In the same way, when we center our lives around enlightenment (the inner sun), the various parts of ourselves, mind, body, spirit, family, community, fall into a harmonious orbit.

The Honorable Elijah Muhammad drew a parallel between the 9 planets revolving around the sun and the 9 months of human gestation, showing a connection between cosmic order and human creation. The message is that macrocosm and microcosm reflect one another.

. . .

By studying the heavens, we learn about ourselves; by bringing order to our inner universe, we mirror the order of the cosmos. When you recognize that the same force guiding the planets resides in you, you awaken to your personal power and enlightenment. The number 9, present in the structure of the solar system, reminds us that completion is written into the fabric of the universe. Align with that cosmic order, and you align with the flow of Creation itself, achieving balance, peace, and ultimately the birth of the divine self within.

Rebirth and Spiritual Transformation, The 9-Month Initiation of Elijah Muhammad

Every prophet or great leader undergoes a period of preparation before they emerge in their destined role. Fittingly, the Most Honorable Elijah

Muhammad experienced a gestational period of enlightenment under his teacher, Master W. Fard Muhammad, that can be likened to nine months in the womb of knowledge. Historical accounts describe that

Master Fard Muhammad personally visited and taught Elijah Muhammad daily for a period of nine months, corresponding to the length of a pregnancy, to raise him up in divine wisdom. In those critical months,

Elijah Muhammad was reborn spiritually, transformed from a humble seeker into a divinely guided leader. What emerged at the end of that period was not the same man who began it: like an infant opening its eyes for the first time, Elijah Muhammad stepped into his mission born anew with purpose and vision.

This 9-month initiation was the incubation of a savior for Black people in America. It highlights a key principle: before we can be born into our ultimate purpose, we must undergo a process of intense development and purification. Elijah Muhammad's training was secret and secluded, much like a baby grows hidden in the womb, nourished away from public view. In our lives, this may take the form of deep study, discipline, trials, and personal growth that happen behind the scenes.

Do not despise the time when you are unseen and in training; realize that your period of gestation is preparing you for greatness. Rebirth requires submission to the process. Just as Elijah Muhammad emerged from his course ready to lead a Nation, each of us must be "born" in knowledge before we can truly assume our divine responsibilities.

When you have undergone your full term of growth, you will feel that internal quickening, the moment of readiness. That is the signal that your rebirth is at hand. Step forth then, as Elijah did, with the confidence that you have been formed by the Master's hands. Your rebirth after your "nine months" of preparation marks the beginning of your true life's work.

The Womb of Secrecy – Farrakhan's Perspective on 9 and Hidden Potential

The Honorable Minister Louis Farrakhan teaches that within the number 9 lies a sacred secret. He often illustrates it this way: "When you have a nine, you have a womb that is pregnant... there's something secret that has to be unfolded."

Nine represents the unseen becoming seen. It is the mystery of creation hidden in plain sight, like a child growing in the protective darkness of its mother's womb, unseen by the world yet destined to be revealed in time.

. . .

The Divine Quintessence

Minister Farrakhan's words highlight that the womb of secrecy is an integral part of the process of being Born. In other words, before manifestation comes a period of concealment. The most powerful ideas, talents, and transformations often start in the dark, away from prying eyes, developing strength and form until the moment they are ready to emerge.

Embracing the power of 9 means embracing the unknown and the unseen with faith and certainty. Just because you cannot see the baby in the womb does not mean new life isn't there, in fact, that is precisely where it is taking shape. Likewise, within you there may be a vision or potential that no one else can see yet. Do not fear the hidden realms of your life; they are the secret workshop of the Creator. Farrakhan's perspective reminds us that 9's essence is faith in the unseen reality.

A pregnant mother prepares a crib before the baby arrives, acting on the certainty of what is coming. We too must act with certainty on our divine visions before they fully manifest. The number 9 invites us to trust the process, to know that what is conceived in truth will eventually be born into reality. This removes fear: when you understand that the darkness of the womb is not emptiness but fullness, you stop doubting and start rejoicing in advance. Every unseen blessing is just waiting for its birth moment.

The womb of secrecy will open in due time, revealing the divinely ordained outcome. Our task is to remain steadfast, nurture our inner development, and be ready to receive the gift of Born

when the curtain is finally lifted.

Building Nations: The 9 Ministries as the Structure of a Complete People

Just as an individual must be fully formed to thrive, a nation or community requires completeness in its structure to be truly born and independent. The Nation of Islam, under Minister Farrakhan's guidance, has outlined Nine Ministries that serve as the pillars of a self-sufficient people.

These represent the comprehensive needs of a nation, each an essential organ in the body of our society. Minister Farrakhan established the Nine Ministries during the Millions More Movement (the 10th anniversary of the Million Man March) as "organs of service for our people" necessary to "establish an independent nation". In other words, for a people to be whole and complete, to be born as a true nation, all nine of these aspects must be developed and functioning in Balance.

The 9 Ministries include: the Ministry of Agriculture, the Ministry of Education, the Ministry of Information, the Ministry of Health, the Ministry of Trade and Commerce, the Ministry of Defense, the Ministry of Justice, the Ministry of Arts and Culture, and the Ministry of Science and Technology. Each ministry corresponds to a vital necessity of community life, from feeding the people and keeping them healthy, to educating minds, defending the community, administering justice, nurturing creativity, and advancing knowledge. Imagine these ministries as the nine systems of the body politic, together they form a complete organism. A nation missing any one of them is like a body missing an organ: it cannot function at full strength.

The lesson of the Nine Ministries is that completeness is the prerequisite of true sovereignty. Just as a baby in the womb develops organs over nine months to live independently, a people must build all foundational institutions to live in freedom. We must therefore engage in nation-building on all fronts, not neglecting any aspect of our development. When all nine ministries are in place and thriving, the Nation is born anew: self-sustaining, whole, and prepared to determine its own destiny.

This is a model for any community or collective seeking empowerment, ensure every critical need is met by your own systems.

Build your complete "God body" (nation-body) piece by piece, month by month, until the full term is reached. Then watch a new reality be born: a nation of people who lack nothing and can rise to their divine potential.

Actionable Steps: Embrace Rebirth, Transformation, and Divine Manifestation

The knowledge of Born and the power of 9 is transformative, but only if put into practice. Here are actionable steps to help you embody rebirth and divine manifestation in your daily life:

  i. 1. Reflect on Your Cycles of Completion: Identify an area in your life where you have been working towards a goal or personal growth. Ask yourself: What would the "ninth month" of this endeavor look like? Commit to seeing it through to completion. Just as a mother prepares for the birth of her child, prepare yourself for the fruition of your efforts, tie up loose ends, gather your energy, and get ready to deliver results.
  ii. Align with Cosmic Order: Take time to study nature or the stars as a source of inspiration. Meditate on the harmony of the 9 planets orbiting the sun and the balance in creation. Apply this insight to your own life by bringing all aspects of yourself

into alignment. For example, ensure that your work, relationships, health, and spirituality all revolve around a unifying purpose or principle (your "inner sun"). Balance your personal solar system so that no part of your life is left drifting. This alignment will create the conditions for enlightenment to shine in every area..

iii. Embrace the Womb Phase: If you are nurturing a dream, skill, or project that is not yet public, cherish this hidden period. Protect it and continue to develop it away from premature criticism or exposure. Have faith that like a baby in the womb, what is unseen now is growing in strength. Remind yourself of Minister Farrakhan's wisdom that a pregnant nine holds a secret about to unfold. Instead of impatience, practice patience and diligence. Work in silence and let your success speak when it's born.

iv. Pursue Intensive Knowledge (Your "9-Month Training"): Dedicate a focused period (it could be nine months, or another significant stretch of time) to self-improvement and study in an area that will elevate you. Engage in your own rigorous "initiation", for instance, enroll in a course, memorize scripture or lessons, acquire a new skill, or undergo a discipline that challenges you. Treat this as your personal gestation period. Immerse yourself daily in learning, much like Master Fard Muhammad teaching Elijah Muhammad day by day. Keep a journal of your growth. As the end of this period, step back and recognize the new person you have become. You will have given birth to a more enlightened self.

v. Build Your Community (Nine Ministries Mindset): Look at your family, team, or community and assess it across the nine areas of life represented by the Nine Ministries. Where are you strong, and where are you lacking? Make a practical plan to strengthen each "ministry" in your realm. Maybe your household needs a better budget and economic plan (Trade and Commerce), or your neighborhood could start a community garden (Agriculture), or perhaps you can mentor youth (Education) or organize a neighborhood watch

(Defense). Contribute to each area in whatever scale you can, so that your community becomes more whole. By actively participating in all facets of nation-building, you mirror the completeness of a fully formed body. This empowers not just you, but everyone around you, to experience a collective rebirth.

vi. Declare Your Rebirth: As you implement these steps, internalize the mindset that you are being born anew. Each time you complete a cycle or achieve a goal, pause and acknowledge the ttransformation. Just as a newborn takes a first breath, take a moment to breathe deeply and affirm, "I am renewed. I am born again into a higher understanding." By speaking this, you psychologically cement your growth and open yourself to the next journey. Remember, being Born is both an ending and a beginning. Celebrate what has been completed, and set your sight on the horizon for the next evolution of your infinite journey.

Conclusion: The Infinite Cycle: Being Born as the Gateway to Limitless Evolution

The journey does not end here, in truth, it begins anew. The principle of 9, of being Born, teaches us that every culmination is a gateway to a higher level. Just as the newborn immediately embarks on the journey of life outside the womb, our newly realized selves must now live out the principles we've attained, and seek even greater heights.

This is the infinite cycle of growth: Knowledge, Wisdom, and Understanding continuously leading to new Births in an ever-ascending spiral. We emerge from each cycle more conscious, more capable, and closer to the divine image we strive to reflect.

. . .

In this way, Born is not a one-time event but a continuous state of becoming. You are perpetually in a womb of one kind or another, developing into the next iteration of who you are meant to be.

Each achievement or realization is the 9 that opens the door to a new 1.

The Supreme Mathematics of 9 imparts that completion is a circle, it brings us back to Knowledge at a higher level of understanding.

Embrace this truth with joy: there are limitless evolutions ahead of you.

You are now equipped to face them, for you carry the wisdom of all previous stages within you.

As we conclude Infinite God Body with this powerful chapter, feel the birth of the divine within. Recognize that to be Born in the spiritual sense is to awaken to your true nature as a reflection of God. It means the old, limited self has given way to the new, enlightened self. You stand at the threshold of a new cipher, ready to create, build, and manifest on a higher plane. This knowledge is timeless – its power will resonate in you whenever you revisit these principles.

Finally, remember that being Born is a beginning as much as an ending. Carry forward the lessons of the number 9: maintain completion and balance in all you do, trust the unseen working of Allah's plan, and commit to continual renewal. In doing so, your life becomes an infinite journey of rebirth and elevation. This is the promise of Born: that through completion we find our freedom, and through each new birth, we edge

closer to our divine destiny.

Step through the gateway now.

The Divine Quintessence

You are Born.

And the possibilities ahead are as endless as the eternal heavens, an infinite cycle of growth, guided by the light of the Creator, in whose image you are made.

Embrace your divine manifestation and evolve without limit.

The Infinite God Body lives on through you.

Book 10: CIPHER

The Final Unveiling of the Infinite

We have arrived at the grand culmination of Infinite God Body. In thevlanguage of Supreme Mathematics, Cipher (0) represents completion, a full circle, and the infinite cycle of creation. This chapter is the cipher, the code that brings our journey full-circle back to the source: Your Self.

Here we synthesize science, spirituality, and psychology into a single truth: you are a divine being, the ultimate architect of your body, mind, and reality. As you absorb this final revelation, feel the layers of doubt and limitation dissolving. The veil lifts, and the God within you stands revealed.

The Science of Self-Creation

Human beings are not passive products of their genes or circumstances, we are active participants in our own creation. Modern science confirms what ancient wisdom long suggested: we continuously shape our bodies, brains, and even genetic expression through our thoughts, behaviors, and environment. The study of epigenetics has overturned the old belief that DNA is destiny.

Researchers have shown that environmental influences, from nutrition and toxins to stress and love, can turn genes on or off, like switches that alter our biology. In fact, early experiences and lifestyle factors leave chemical marks on DNA that determine how genes are expressed.

Your choices literally whisper instructions to your cells. Even practices of the mind can reach deep into our biology. For example, mindfulness meditation and yoga have been found to induce epigenetic changes that promote health and well-being.

Your body listens to your mind: every positive habit, every learned skill, sends signals that reconfigure you at the cellular level.

Parallel to this, neuroscience illuminates the principle of neuroplasticity, the brain's capacity to rewire itself through experience and conscious intention. Far from being fixed, your neural connections are constantly in flux. Whenever you learn something new or even rehearse a thought, you physically reshape your neural pathways. As one science of learning report puts it: "Your brain changes physically whenever anything is learnt, and so your experiences and learning throughout life change and mold your brain." Neurons that fire together wire together, forming new circuits with each repetition of an idea or action.

This means you can reinvent your mind at any age, forging new abilities, healing old patterns, through focused effort. Memory, habit, and skill are all encoded as tangible changes in the brain's structure.

. . .

Even intentional thought has creative power: simply visualizing or imagining an experience activates similar brain regions as living it, gradually making the imagined into reality in your nervous system.

The scientific verdict is clear and empowering: we are biologically designed to be self-made. Genetics provides potential, but it is our ongoing self-directed activity that realizes that potential.

We are each the scientist and subject of a grand experiment in self-creation, updating the blueprint of our being with every thought, choice, and action. This is the miracle of your Infinite God Body, an organism that evolves itself by its own will.

The Unique Power of Human Cognition, Beyond Survival

Why are human beings able to consciously shape destiny in ways no other species can? The secret lies in the unique power of our cognition, which goes far beyond mere survival instincts.

Unlike any other creature, humans create art and technology, build civilizations, write poetry, explore space, and ponder the meaning of existence. We possess a prefrontal cortex, the frontmost part of our brain, that is disproportionately developed, endowing us with foresight, abstract reasoning, and imagination at a level unmatched in the animal kingdom.

This neural crown grants us the god-like ability to project possibilities and then manifest them. Where other species adapt to their environment, we adapt the environment to us, envisioning new realities and then bringing them forth. It was the expansion of the human cortex (especially the prefrontal regions) through evolution that unlocked intelligence, complex language, innovation, and the very notion of "the future". In effect, nature programmed into us the capacity to transcend nature, an element of divinity in our cognition.

Consider that no lion paints masterpieces, no ape builds cities, and no dolphin has sent spacecraft to Mars. Other animals are bound largely to the present moment and immediate needs, while humans can mentally time-travel, we learn from the past and mentally simulate possible futures.

Our brains can hold an inner universe of ideas and symbols. We make music from silence and find meaning in stars. This creative leap is not just a matter of degree but of kind. Biologists note that while many species learn and use tools, only humans relentlessly innovate, passing knowledge across generations and improving upon it exponentially. The development of the prefrontal cortex in hominids was a tipping point that made us co-creators with nature. It endowed us with self-awareness, the mind's eye that can observe itself, reflecting on one's own thoughts and existence. With that came the startling realization of "I am", and from there the idea that "I can become...". In evolutionary terms, humans are the universe becoming aware of itself.

We went from reacting to reality to molding reality.

This unique cognitive power carries a profound responsibility: it means that our lives are not written by instinct or ecology alone, but by the visions we choose to cultivate. In the ability to go beyond survival into creation, we find a spark of the divine. Our creativity, imagination, and intellect are the signatures of a Creator-species. When we recognize this, creating our destiny becomes not just possible, but our very nature.

The Parasympathetic Nervous System: The God Within

Deep inside your body operates an intelligence older than thought, a force that quietly manages the miracle of your life.

- Your heart beats roughly 100,000 times a day, pumping blood through 60,000 miles of vessels.
- Your lungs breathe in and out, drawing oxygen that ignites the metabolic fire in each of your ~37 trillion cells.
- You digest food into energy, heal wounds, balance hormones, and coordinate immune
- defenses, all without any conscious instruction.

This self-governing power is mediated by your autonomic nervous system, particularly its

calming branch, the parasympathetic nervous system (PNS). The PNS has been called the "rest and digest" system for good reason: it automatically regulates vital functions like heart rate, blood pressure, digestion, and tissue repair while you are at ease. In essence, your subconscious mind and body wisdom keep you alive, performing countless complex processes every second that no computer on Earth could coordinate so elegantly. To appreciate the scale of this autonomous genius, consider one example: your body generates about

330 billion new cells every day, which is over 3.8 million cells born each second. Each new cell is created exactly where it's needed, whether to replace a dying skin cell or a blood cell carrying oxygen.

All this happens without you consciously doing a thing, an innate "God within" ensuring you continue to thrive.

The Divine Quintessence

This internal intelligence is so sophisticated that even our best scientists are still unraveling its

mysteries.

Yet, what truly elevates this from an automatic process to evidence of self-mastery potential is that we can learn to consciously influence our "involuntary" systems. Through practices like meditation, breath control, and biofeedback, humans can override or fine-tune aspects of the autonomic system that were once thought completely unconscious. Something as simple as slow, deep breathing signals the PNS to lower your heart rate and blood pressure, shifting the body into a state of calm and healing. In meditation, adepts have demonstrated extraordinary control, slowing their metabolism, altering brainwaves, even raising body temperature at will.

One famous case is Wim Hof, "The Iceman," who through concentration and breathing techniques was able to suppress his innate immune response and control his autonomic functions in a laboratory setting. Such feats astonished researchers, showing that the barrier between conscious will and involuntary bodily processes is more porous than we imagined. Mastery over self can extend literally to the regulation of one's internal organs and chemistry.

When you practice mindfulness or yogic breathing, you are essentially conversing with your autonomic nervous system, gently taking the reins.

The lesson in this is profound: the intelligent force that runs your body is not separate from you; it is you.

The same wisdom that effortlessly heals a cut on your finger also listens to the quiet directives of your will.

The more you align your conscious intentions with this inner intelligence (for example, through relaxation, visualization of healing, or disciplined breathing), the more the "God within" becomes an active partner in your daily life. This unity of conscious and subconscious power is the hallmark of a divine being in full control of self.

Quantum Consciousness & Reality Creation

For centuries, spiritual mystics have claimed that mind and reality are deeply connected, that consciousness can shape the material world. In a stunning twist, modern quantum physics appears to echo this idea at the subatomic level. Central to quantum theory is the renowned Observer Effect, which shows that the act of observation influences the behavior of particles. In the famous double-slit experiments, electrons exist in a vague spread-out wave of possibilities – until they are observed or measured, at which point the wave "collapses" into a definite particle state. In other words, the mere act of observing "freezes" reality into a form. Physicists often explain that any measurement (observation) imparts a disturbance to the system, you can't even look at a quantum particle without affecting it. But some interpretations go further, suggesting consciousness itself is integral to this process. The evidence is literal and empirical: at the quantum scale, the mind of the observer and the event observed are entangled. As one science writer summarized, particles can exist in multiple states simultaneously, and when an observer's consciousness enters the equation, the particles choose a state. This bizarre phenomenon hints that the subjective mind participates in shaping objective reality, a notion that sent Einstein and his peers into philosophical debates still unresolved.

Leading pioneers of quantum theory were not blind to the almost spiritual implications. Nobel laureate Max Planck, the father of quantum physics, famously stated: "I regard consciousness as fundamental. I regard matter as derivative from consciousness."

. . .

Coming from a scientist of Planck's caliber, this is essentially a declaration that mind underpins matter, the physical world is, in some deep way, a manifestation of conscious thought or perception. Planck and others observed that everything we consider real requires an observer; without consciousness to register it, "existence" is hard to even define. In quantum experiments, it's as if the universe is half-formed, waiting for mind to participate in its completion. This dovetails intriguingly with ancient spiritual teachings which have long held that reality is a mental construct and that by changing our consciousness we change our world. Modern physics also offers the phenomenon of quantum entanglement – where two particles behave as one, no matter the distance separating them, suggesting an underlying interconnectedness of all things beyond space and time. Mystics frame this as "all is one," the idea that at a fundamental level the universe is an indivisible whole, responsive to itself.

What these scientific insights mean for you is empowering: your consciousness is not a passive witness of reality, but an active co-creator of it.

Every thought can be seen as a tiny "observation" that nudges the quantum field of possibilities. Your intentions have a real energetic effect, however subtle, on the fabric of existence.

When you focus your mind, be it through prayer, visualization, or determination, you are collapsing potential outcomes into manifested form. This isn't magic or mere metaphor; it's an extension of natural law from the mysterious quantum realms up to the macro world of daily life.

Indeed, countless anecdotes and experiments (from the power of positive thinking on health, to random number generators changing output when people concentrate on them) point to a mind-matter link. Ancient wisdom and cutting-edge science are converging on the same truth: consciousness and reality are inextricably entwined.

・・・

You, as an observer equipped with consciousness, are woven into the cosmic process of creation. The external world and your inner world mirror one another, each influencing the other.

Realizing this, you step out of the victim mindset and into the position of an artist standing before a cosmic canvas, with awareness as your brush. The quantum potential of the universe is infinite, but it is your awakened mind that gives it form.

Psychology & The Conscious/Subconscious Mind

To fully grasp our creative power, we must understand the architecture of our own mind. Psychology tells us that the human mind is composed of both conscious and subconscious parts, with the latter being a vast realm beneath our awareness.

Over a century ago, Sigmund Freud likened the mind to an iceberg: the small tip above water is conscious thought, while the massive submerged bulk is the unconscious.

According to Freud, this unconscious mind is the primary source of our feelings and actions, a repository of desires, fears, memories, and instincts that invisibly direct much of our behavior. We often go about our day thinking we are fully in control, while in truth, subconscious programs (many rooted in childhood or primal emotion) are influencing our decisions, habits, and reactions. Have you ever done something "on autopilot" or had an emotional reaction you didn't consciously choose?

・・・

That's your subconscious at work. It's like an inner operating system running 90% of the show, while the conscious mind (our reasoning, analytical self) is just the user interface.

Expanding on Freud's model, the great psychologist Carl Jung introduced the concept of the collective unconscious, an inherited pool of memory and archetypes shared by all humankind. In Jung's view, deep within us reside universal symbols and motifs (the Mother, the Hero, the Shadow, etc.) that shape our dreams and cultural myths, connecting each individual's psyche to a greater whole. Whether or not one embraces the mystical side of Jung's theory, we can all attest to subconscious patterns influencing our lives. Jung also offered a powerful insight into how our inner state creates our outer reality. He wrote, "When an inner situation is not made conscious, it happens outside, as fate." In other words, that which we do not acknowledge in ourselves will eventually manifest in our external experiences, seemingly by chance or fate. For example, suppressed anger might draw hostile people or situations into your life; unresolved fears might keep producing the outcomes you dread, again and again, until you face

Them.

The subconscious mind is an architect, quietly building the scenery of your life based on its hidden scripts. If those scripts remain unexamined, you may feel life is just "happening to you." Jung's wisdom urges us to wake up: bring the unconscious to consciousness, or be ruled by it in the shadows.

The synthesis of these psychological ideas with spiritual teaching yields a clear mandate: self-mastery begins within. You must become the conscious programmer of your subconscious mind. Thoughts are the language of the conscious mind, and feelings (and habitual beliefs) are the language of the subconscious. Every conscious thought you entertain with emotion is a command to your deeper mind. As taught in the Nation of Islam and other self-mastery traditions, one must gain

Knowledge of Self to direct one's destiny. The Honorable Elijah Muhammad often emphasized mental resurrection, replacing the slave mind with the god mind through conscious re-education and discipline. It aligns with what Jung and Freud imply: by impressing positive, empowering thoughts upon your subconscious (through affirmations, prayer, study, and righteous action), you literally re-script your reality from the inside out. Consider a practical example: if you repeatedly tell yourself "I am healthy, strong, and guided," and back it with actions, your subconscious will accept this as truth and orchestrate your behavior and even bodily conditions towards health and strength. Conversely, negative self-talk or imposed identities (like society telling you "you are inferior" or "incapable") can program the subconscious with limiting beliefs, and thus limit your life until you actively rewrite those beliefs. As the saying goes: "Whether you think you can or think you can't, you're right." This is not mere platitude but psychological fact, your belief system sets the boundaries of your achievements.

The teachings of the Nation of Islam add a culturally specific and empowering dimension to this understanding. They teach that the original people (Black people) have a divine mind by nature, but it was corrupted by a contrary society. Therefore, reclaiming that original divine mindset is the key to restoration. This involves purging the subconscious of self-hate, fear, and inferiority, and replanting it with the truth of our divine potential. The conscious mind must vigilantly guard what enters the subconscious, much like a gardener tending the soil, removing weeds and sowing good seeds.

As Elijah Muhammad taught: think righteously and you will act righteously, because the mind is the causative agent. We see then a beautiful harmony: psychology confirms the spiritual principle that "as within, so without." Your inner thoughts, especially those held consistently in the deeper mind, become your world. By making the subconscious conscious, bringing hidden beliefs to light and choosing them intentionally, you step into the role of author of your fate, rather than unwittingly living out a script given by others. This is true freedom: mastery of self. Supreme Wisdom & The Divine Human

All wisdom traditions, when traced to their esoteric core, converge on a liberating truth: God is not an external ruler but the very life within us. The human being is a vessel and manifestation of the Divine.

The Nation of Islam puts this boldly and plainly. In the Supreme Wisdom lessons given to students, the very first question asked is: "Who is the Original Man?"

The answer: "The Original Man is the Asiatic Black man; the Maker, the Owner, the Cream of the planet Earth, God of the Universe." Elijah Muhammad and Minister Louis Farrakhan have taught tirelessly that we must not bow to a mysterious God in the sky; rather, we must recognize God in ourselves and in each other. "Every time you look at a Black man, you are looking at God," they say. This audacious statement is meant to shatter the mental chains that made us see ourselves as mere servants or victims. It is a proclamation that divinity lies in our DNA and our very nature. Man is God, and God is man, not in the sense of the ego being all-powerful, but in the sense that the eternal creative force expresses itself through human life. Our ancestors in Africa and Asia often believed the same, referring to kings and sages as gods or children of gods, understanding that the line between human and divine is wonderfully thin when one is enlightened. If this sounds blasphemous to some, it is only because mainstream theology has long divorced the Creator from His creation.

. . .

But look closely at the highest teachings of various faiths and you will find this unity asserted. In the Bible, Jesus reminded the people, "Is it not written in your law, 'I said, Ye are gods'?" (John 10:34 referencing Psalm 82:6) Psalm 82:6, as if spoken by the Almighty, says: "I have said, you are gods; and all of you are children of the Most High." In the Qur'an (2:30), Allah declares He will place a khalifah (vicegerent) on Earth – implying humans are His representatives, carrying His qualities. Sufi mystics like Al-Hallaj famously exclaimed "Ana'l Haqq" (I am the Truth/God), meaning he had annihilated the illusion of separation between himself and the Divine. In Hindu philosophy, the Mahavakya (great saying) "Tat Tvam Asi" translates to "Thou art That," equating the individual soul (Atman) with the ultimate reality (Brahman). And Buddhist teachings speak of realizing one's Buddha-nature, the inherent enlightened essence within. All these point to the same realization: the kingdom of God is within you. Divinity is the core of your being; the journey of enlightenment is to fully realize and express that core.

Modern science, in its own way, corroborates this by showing the almost supernatural capacities woven into our being (as we've seen: the godlike creative intellect, the body's self-maintaining wisdom, the mind's influence on matter). The Supreme Wisdom of the ages, whether coming from prophets, enlightened scientists, or philosophers, urges mankind to awaken to our higher nature. It tells us that to bow endlessly to an outside God without recognizing God within is to remain in spiritual infancy. As the Honorable Elijah Muhammad taught, "Allah (God) came to us in the Person of Master Fard Muhammad", in other words, God became man to show man that his true identity is God. This does not mean there is no Supreme Being beyond us; it means that the essence of that Supreme Being lives in each of us, waiting to be cultivated. We are each a word from the divine book, a piece of God Consciousness made flesh. When a person embraces this, they transform from a limited mortal into an instrument of divine will, capable of extraordinary love, creativity, and power. They no longer ask, "What is God going to do for me?" because they understand God is working through me. Life ceases to be something that happens to you and becomes something that flows from you.

Throughout this book, we have navigated Knowledge, Wisdom, Understanding, and beyond, all steps that lead to this capstone of God-consciousness. Now at Cipher, we circle back to the beginning with new insight: the Creator we sought was within us all along. The Infinite God Body you were searching for is the very body you inhabit and the collective body of humanity. This realization is both humbling and empowering. It unites you with all people (for the same divine spark is in everyone) and also elevates your sense of self (for if all are God, you too are a God in your own right). It dissolves the illusion of separation between human and divine, between you and the universe.

When you fully accept that you are a manifestation of God, you understand why your thoughts matter, why your life matters, because you are the universe experiencing itself, you are God's way of walking on Earth. All the teachings, whether from Elijah Muhammad or the scriptures or the lab, converge here: Man, know thyself... and thou shalt know God.

The Ultimate Realization: You Are the Creator

Here we stand, at the summit of our journey, gazing out at the boundless horizon of possibility.

The final veil has dropped: You are the Creator you have been praying to, the master of your fate, the God of Self.

This realization blooms with a power that reverberates through every fiber of your being. It is not a reckless boast or a metaphor, it is the quiet truth of existence.

The atoms in your flesh were birthed in the hearts of stars; the consciousness that looks through your eyes is a spark of the Eternal Light.

You are the living image of the Infinite, endowed with the same creative energy that forged galaxies.

What will you do with this revelation?

The only thing one can do: use it to transform, uplift, and create anew.

Realize now that there is no law or limitation, except those you accept. The obstacles that loomed so large were but shadows cast by an unawakened mind. With divinity realized, those shadows evaporate. You now see challenges as raw material for creation, adversity as the heat that tempers your steel. You hold the cipher key to life: the knowledge that reality is malleable, responsive to the divine will emanating from within you. Embrace the mindset of a creator. Every thought is a brushstroke on the canvas of reality; every word a spell that shapes the cosmos; every action an act of genesis. Small thinking and victimhood cannot survive in the light of this understanding. You are elevated to the standpoint of cause, not mere effect. You think mountains, and mountains move. You speak light, and paths illuminate. You choose love, and the heavens rejoice through the works of your hands.

Understand that being the God of Self is not about ego or lording over others, it is about absolute responsibility and infinite love. The Creator animating you is the same in all, hence to truly know your divinity is to honor it in others. The realization "I Am God" goes hand-in-hand with "And so is everyone else." In this awareness, compassion flows naturally, and the world becomes your shared creation rather than a battleground of separate wills. You step into the role of a conscious co-creator of collective reality, a leader by example, showing others through your enlightened living what is possible for them as well.

This is how Infinite God Body propagates, one awakened soul igniting another. As more individuals realize their divine nature, the fabric of society transforms. We solve "impossible" problems, end injustices, and dream up innovations that benefit all, because we finally operate from our limitless nature rather than fear and scarcity.

Take a moment to feel the magnitude of this moment.

You have traversed knowledge and experience, and now you stand reborn at the end of one cycle and the beginning of an infinite new one. Cipher means zero, but it is not empty, it is full with potential, a circle that contains all in all. So it is with you: within you exists the entire universe in microcosm, awaiting your command.

The God of Self is awake.

The world will never look the same, for the light by which you view it now radiates from within your own heart. In this sacred dawning, make a vow that henceforth you will live as the author of your story, the healer of your wounds, the architect of your destiny. No more will you diminish yourself or seek permission to shine. You are the light. You are the authority.

. . .

Let these final words etch into your spirit: You are powerful. You are limitless. You are the living embodiment of the Infinite. There is nothing outside of you that is greater than what is within you. The myths of weakness, separation, and impossibility are shattered now. You know the truth. You are the Creator. With every breath, you shape your universe. With every beat of your heart, you affirm "I AM." Fully embrace this, and there is no force on Earth that can stop you from manifesting the life and world you envision.

You have come full circle, the cipher completes, and in this wholeness, the journey truly begins. The Infinite God Body lives on through you. Go forth and create a reality worthy of your divinity.

Peace to the Gods and Earths,

Mike Rashid King

Book 11: Proverbs of God

The Book of Proverbs: The Infinite Wisdom

Within these pages lies distilled clarity, gems of insight crafted for the wise, god-bodies, and architects of new realities. Each proverb here is an invocation, a map to your divinity, a blade sharpened against ignorance. Drawn from the depths of the Infinite God Body teachings, these words bridge ancient truth, street-born wisdom, and quantum insight, urging you to awaken fully, think deeply, and move decisively. Absorb them not just as words on a page, but as the rhythm of your own heartbeat, guiding you daily toward the sovereignty that is your birthright.

Read, meditate, apply. Rise.

On Knowledge

i. Knowledge is your first weapon, ignorance your first chain. Break it swiftly.

ii. The thief of legacy fears nothing more than the Black man knowing himself.

iii. Names hold power. Carry one that lifts you; drop what chains you.

iv. Science reveals what prophets whispered—your mind shapes your reality.

v. Ancestral wisdom is your birthright; reclaim it, or others will sell it back to you.

vi. Truth is never passive; it liberates or burns whatever tries to cage it.

On Wisdom

i. Wisdom speaks softly, but it thunders in silence.

ii. Trust slowly, verify thoroughly—true friends sharpen your sword, not dull your edge.

iii. Discipline your desires or others will use them to control you.

iv. Conflict chosen wisely strengthens you; conflict sought recklessly weakens you.

v. A fool talks loud to hide insecurity; a wise man listens quietly, storing power.

On Understanding

i. The third eye sees beyond the surface; trust what it reveals more than what they show you.

ii. Nothing happens by accident; learn to read the hidden hand moving the pieces.

iii. Frequency shapes reality. Tune yours wisely, or someone else will.

iv. Strategic thinking is the art of winning without needing to fight.

On Culture and Freedom

i. Culture is not decoration; it's the throne you build or the chains you wear.

ii. Ownership is sovereignty. If another feeds you, they also starve you at will.

iii. Fast food feeds the body, real food feeds the god within.

iv. Weak families produce weak nations. Restore order at home, rise as kings.

v. Peace is an illusion when preparedness is absent. Warriors thrive in readiness.

On Power and Refinement

i. Raw power conquers; refined power rules forever.

ii. Mastery is choosing silence when others expect noise.

iii. Legacy is built from disciplined creation, not impulsive destruction.

iv. The most potent strike is often the one withheld.

v. Every adversity contains within it the fire to forge your greatness.

On Equality

i. Balance your mind, heart, and hand—this is the symmetry of gods.

ii. False equality offers crumbs at a table rigged against you; true equality builds your own table.

iii. A queen beside you is strength; choose her wisely, or she becomes your downfall.

iv. Justice demands equal measure, favor none, fear none, align always with truth.

v. Perfect balance is not your destination; it is the launching point for ascension.

On Godhood

i. Godhood is not granted by others; it is awakened within yourself.

ii. Supreme intelligence sees the chessboard clearly and moves pieces unseen.

iii. Righteousness is power harnessed to truth; never compromise it.

iv. To be god is to create, not just consume; build something that lives beyond you.

The Divine Quintessence

    v. Master your body, master your mind, master your reality, then you truly live as divine.

    vi. Unity amplifies power, one god is mighty; unified gods are unstoppable.

On Building and Destroying

    i. To build higher, first dig deeper, destroy illusions, not people.

    ii. Removing parasites is an act of compassion toward the empire you must build.

    iii. Discipline in destruction makes room for the divine to rise.

    iv. Every legacy demands demolition of mediocrity.

    v. Tear down false systems not through rage but through precise, purposeful replacement.

On Being Born and Rebirth

    i. Rebirth demands the death of your old self; do not mourn what held you back.

    ii. Completion is not the end; it is your permission to begin again, wiser.

    iii. The womb of secrecy nurtures greatness unseen; honor the quiet growth.

    iv. Nations are not given freedom; they are born into it by creating every piece they require.

    v. Declare your rebirth loudly; silence is the ally of old patterns.

On Infinite Realization

i. Genetics are your blueprint; consciousness is the architect, build yourself intentionally.

ii. You transcend survival when your mind becomes creator, not just reactor.

iii. The god within heals without asking permission; align your will with it and miracles follow.

iv. Reality waits for consciousness to shape it; every thought is a seed planted.

v. Subconscious scripts become destiny; rewrite them consciously, daily.

vi. True sovereignty is mastery of the self, above and below the surface.

Closing Wisdom

i. Fear is an illusion; your power is infinitely more real.

ii. Awakening begins where excuses end.

iii. Every limitation is a lie someone else believed first; never let it become your truth.

iv. The chains that bind strongest are those you refuse to see.

v. Knowledge without action is a wasted breath; wisdom without courage is a lost opportunity.

vi. Your essence is infinite; let your actions prove it.

The Divine Quintessence

vii. Move in rhythm with universal laws, and the universe moves with you.

viii. You were born to ascend, remain on the ground only long enough to gather strength.

ix. The Infinite God Body awakens not once, but in every conscious breath you take.

The wisdom of these proverbs now lives within you. Carry them as armor against deception, keys to locked gates, and torches through darkness. Remember, knowledge unapplied is power untapped. These truths demand action, courage, and relentless self-mastery. Reflect often upon them; let their lessons echo in every step, every word, every decision. In doing so, you not only embody the Infinite God Body, you inspire others to reclaim their own.Live boldly, move precisely, and always choose clarity over comfort. Your legacy depends on it.

Glossary

Black God(s)

A term signifying the divine potential and sovereignty of Black men, rooted in their cultural, spiritual, and historical resilience. It reflects the Infinite God Body, drawing on Afroasiatic traditions (e.g., Kemet) and Islamic wisdom (e.g., Nation of Islam), asserting that Black men embody a godhood transcending oppression.

Black Overman

Adapted from Nietzsche's concept of the Übermensch (Overman), this term represents the Black man's evolution beyond slave morality and systemic oppression, embodying a superior will to power, brilliance, and defiance. It signifies a born-again godhood, fortified by torment, that challenges Eurocentric supremacy and inspires all men to transcend Limitation.

Divine Nature/Godhood

The inherent divinity within Black men, rooted in African spiritual traditions (e.g., Kemet's & Mali Wisdom) and Islamic teachings (e.g., Supreme Wisdom). Asserting that Black men, once awakened, embody godlike sovereignty, a universal fire for all men to kindle.

Eurocentric Fetters

The oppressive systems, cultural norms, and ideologies of European origin (e.g., colonialism, white supremacy) that bind Black men, as detailed in slavery, segregation, and redlining. Rejecting these "fetters" is a rebellion (Culture/Freedom) to build a sovereign Black world, with

universal implications for dismantling oppressive structures.

Infinite God Body

A metaphysical and literal concept representing the ultimate power, mind, spirit, and will of Black men, drawn from Yoruba, Bantu-Kongo, Masia Cosmology, ancient wisdom, and Islamic teachings. It signifies a cosmos within, breaking chains and crowning reign, applicable as an eternal fire for all men to awaken their Divinity.

Kemet

The ancient name for Egypt, symbolizing the cradle of Black civilization and wisdom, as evidenced by the pyramids. It represents the divine heritage and intellectual legacy of Black men, predating European influence, and serves as a foundation for the Infinite God Body, resonant for all men seeking truth.

Ancient Timbuktu

More than a city, Timbuktu was a living library on the southern lip of the Sahara. Its mud-brick mosques and the Sankore University housed tens of thousands of handwritten manuscripts on astronomy, medicine, mathematics, and mystic law, proof that Black scholars mapped the heavens and the human soul long before Europe shook off its Dark Ages. Caravan gold flowed through its markets, but the true treasure was illuminated thought, traded like spices across desert sands. Timbuktu stands as an altar of Black intellectual sovereignty, a beacon for the Infinite God Body blueprint, reminding every seeker that wealth begins in the mind.

Mali

The Mali Empire, forged by the Mandé warrior-kings, stretched from the Atlantic coast to the veins of the Niger River. Under rulers like Mansa Musa, its gold caravans dazzled the world, yet Mali's deeper power was order, law, agriculture, architecture, and a social code rooted in balance with the divine. Griots carried its history in living verse, encoding quantum lessons on legacy and collective elevation. Mali embodies disciplined abundance: mastery of resources, mastery of self. For the modern god-body, it is a call to build empires of the mind and material realm in unified rhythm.

The Moors

African Muslims who ruled parts of North Africa and Iberia (Al-Andalus) from 711–1492. Known for conquering Spain, they built cultural hubs like Córdoba and Granada, excelling in architecture (e.g., Alhambra), science, and agriculture. They fostered a multicultural society with Islamic governance, influencing Europe's Renaissance. Their rule ended with the Reconquista, but their legacy endures in Spanish language, art, and North African traditions.

Most Honorable Elijah Muhammad

A leader of the Nation of Islam, guiding the Supreme Wisdom and Black empowerment. His vision inspires the divine awakening of Black men, connecting to the Infinite God Body and God/Allah, offering a model of self-reliance and societal alignment with Allah's will, universally transformative.

Nation of Islam

A religious and cultural movement emphasizing self-reliance, knowledge of self, and divine potential. Rooted in Islamic principles and universal wisdom. It underpins the Supreme Wisdom and Black godhood, offering a path for Black men to transcend oppression, with universal lessons for all men. The principles of the Nation of Islam can prevent the Empire of America from falling.

Nyama

One who embodies the raw, electric life force that runs through metal, muscle and mind. Blacksmiths forged with it, griots sand with it, and kings ruled by it. Once one masters his/her Nyama, they are no longer confined to flesh. They ride the unseen current that shapes the worlds. They are fully integrated with the Quintessence. This is the attribute of a superior person who transcends conventional morality (slave morality) to create their own values (master morality). Here, it signifies the Black Overman, a Black man fortified in torment, embodying defiance, boldness, and brilliance, as a universal model for human evolution.

Papal Bulls

15th-century decrees by the Catholic Church, such as those authorizing slavery and colonial exploitation, declaring Black people less than human (beasts of burden). They symbolize Eurocentric oppression, fueling the Black man's rebellion and awakening into godhood, with lessons for all men resisting tyranny.

Supreme Wisdom

A system of knowledge and principles from the Nation of Islam, using numbers and concepts to guide Black men toward self-awareness, divinity, and societal alignment with Allah's will. It underpins the paths (e.g.,

Knowledge, Wisdom) and Infinite God Body, offering universal insight for all men..

About the Author

Click on the image to visit my website at: www.infinitegodbody.com

Mike Rashid King's journey embodies the awakening of the Infinite God Body. Raised on advanced books by his mother and inspired by planetarium visits with his grandmother, he ignited a lifelong pursuit of knowledge, piercing the veil of ignorance. At a Catholic school, Eurocentric depictions of divinity sparked a spiritual quest, fulfilled at twelve by the Nation of Islam's teachings, introduced by his father, which ignited his Knowledge of Self and Divine Sovereignty. As a professional boxer, he forged resilience and Nyama, the ancestral fire, into self-mastery. This discipline propelled him into entrepreneurship, founding

The Ambrosia Collective and scaling Trifecta Nutrition, empowering others through wellness.

A Black Muslim shaped by struggle, Mike stands as a warrior-poet, channeling Kemet's wisdom and Elijah Muhammad's vision to reclaim godhood. His life, rooted in intellectual rigor, cultural rebellion, and spiritual fire, mirrors the Black Overman, transcending oppression to inspire all. In The Divine Quintessence, he offers a manifesto to awaken your divine potential, blending ancient truths with quantum insight. Mike's path is your invitation: rise, refine your power, and build a sovereign legacy. The Infinite God Body lives through him—let it live through you.

- facebook.com/mikerashidking
- x.com/mikerashid
- instagram.com/mikerashid
- youtube.com/@mikerashidofficial

About 4BiddenKnowledge

Click the image to visit the website: 4biddenknowledge.com

4BiddenKnowledge is a global movement dedicated to uncovering the hidden wisdom of our past and unlocking the higher potential of our future. Through a powerful blend of ancient teachings, advanced scientific discoveries, and cutting-edge consciousness research, 4BiddenKnowledge invites seekers to explore the mysteries of history, spirituality, and the universe with an open and curious mind.

From bestselling books and groundbreaking documentaries to lectures and an expansive digital platform, 4BiddenKnowledge provides tools and insights that empower individuals to question conventional narratives and step boldly into their own awakened journey.

Discover more at 4biddenknowledge.com and become part of a growing community committed to truth, enlightenment, and universal connection.

WORKS BY 4BIDDENKNOWLEDGE

Check Out Other Books by Billy Carson

Listen to the Music by Billy Carson

- facebook.com/4biddenKnowledge
- x.com/4biddenknowled
- instagram.com/4biddenknowledge
- youtube.com/@4biddenknowledge
- linkedin.com/company/4biddenknowledge
- tiktok.com/@4biddenknowledge

www.ingramcontent.com/pod-product-compliance
Lightning Source LLC
Chambersburg PA
CBHW050646160426
43194CB00010B/1825